KANSAS CITY STYLE

Restaurants, Markets, Recipes & Traditions

Ardie A. Davis

Globe
Pequot

GUILFORD, CONNECTICUT

For my family, with all my love

Globe Pequot

An imprint of Rowman & Littlefield

Distributed by NATIONAL BOOK NETWORK

Copyright © 2016 by Ardie A. Davis

All photography © 2015 by Ardie A. Davis

Cartoon on page vii © Charlie Podrebarac

British Library Cataloguing in Publication Information available

Library of Congress Cataloging-in-Publication Data

Davis, Ardie A., author.
  Barbecue lover's Kansas City style / Ardie A. Davis.
      pages cm
  Includes index.
  ISBN 978-1-4930-0158-3 (pbk. : alk. paper) - ISBN 978-1-4930-2378-3 (ebook)
  1. Restaurants—Missouri—Kansas City Region—Guidebooks. 2. Restaurants—Kansas—Kansas City Region—Guidebooks. 3. Barbecuing-Missouri—Kansas City Region—Guidebooks. 4. Barbecuing—Kansas—Kansas City Region—Guidebooks. I. Title.
  TX907.3.M82D38 2015
  647.95778'411—dc23
                                                                    2015031050

♾™ The paper used in this publication meets the minimum requirements of American National Standard for Information Sciences—Permanence of Paper for Printed Library Materials, ANSI/NISO Z39.48-1992.

CONTENTS

ACKNOWLEDGMENTS

While doing the hands-on research; visiting with Kansas City pitmasters; restaurant staff; eating enough barbecue meat and sides to merit a scolding from our family doctor, Tom Snodell; and especially as I wrote this book, I channeled the Kansas City barbecue greats, past and present, for guidance, inspiration, and encouragement. Writing about Kansas City barbecue is a tall order. So many people love our barbecue. They will read this book with a critical eye, expecting me to do justice to the city and the barbecue they know and love. When I measure up to those high expectations, all credit is due to the collective spirit of our entire barbecue community. When I fall short of expectations, it's entirely on my shoulders.

Special thanks to my immediate family for encouragement and patience when writing and research had to take priority: Gretchen, Sarah, Lee, Alan, Kelli, Zachary, Henry, Emma, Elliott, Elise, Barbara, Kathy, and Brad.

Friends who deserve special thanks include:

Gary Berbiglia, former co-owner of Arthur Bryant's, for accompanying me on some of the barbecue adventures, and for letting me pick his brain for hours on various occasions, about past and present Kansas City barbecue history. Gary is a font of knowledge on the subject and an expert in the field.

Chef Paul Kirk, KC Baron of Barbecue, co-author of the America's Best BBQ series of books we wrote for Andrews McMeel. Chef Paul was of great help with some of the recipes and insights on the Kansas City barbecue scene.

Jill Silva, food editor at the Kansas City Star, who introduced Slap's to me and persuaded me to write a weekly *KC Star Chow Town* blog on barbecue. It has been fun and enlightening.

Kirsty Melville, head of the book division at Andrews McMeel, my principal publisher, for giving the okay to do this book for Globe Pequot.

Dennis Hayes, my agent at BarnDance Productions, for recommending me to Globe Pequot and for his always helpful guidance and encouragement.

Michael Gross, senior staff attorney and barbecue aficionado at The Authors Guild, for contract guidance, encouragement, and barbecue insights. Johnny White deserves special thanks for shipping his Kansas City–style ribs to Michael in New York City for a nostalgic feast that reminded Michael of the ribs his dad used to bring home from the former 7th Street Barbecue in Kansas City, Kansas. Of course Johnny's ribs were better.

Thanks to the many Kansas City barbecue pitmasters and restaurant owners who are recognized in this book. You are the reason Kansas City continues to be famous for barbecue.

All of the First Wednesday at Johnny's barbecue lunch group. It would fill a page to name everyone, but you know you're appreciated.

Guy Simpson, KC Rib Doctor, for giving me a bright idea, light bulb crowned Derby hat. It worked like magic when I was stuck for ideas.

Terry Lee, longtime friend, was game to partake of enormous amounts of great Kansas City barbecue with me during the early stages of research. I am forever grateful.

Special thanks to my friend, Gary Bronkema, for sharing the lion's share of on-site research for this project. Gary's GPS—we named her "Daisy"—and OnStar tools got us to the right place at the right time and saved my geographically challenged self from enacting Daddy Bert's, my maternal grandfather's, prediction that I will someday get lost and never find my way back home.

Finally, a huge thanks to Amy Lyons at Globe Pequot for asking me to write this book, and for her exemplary editing and unbounding patience to see it through from concept to reality. Kudos and thanks also to Stephanie Scott at Globe Pequot for outstanding editing.

This was truly a labor of love. I want you to enjoy it.

Hickory Log Bar-B-Q

INTRODUCTION

"Welcome to Barbecue Central, the World Capital of Barbecue—Ground Zero: where it began, where it was perfected, and where it reigns supreme above all others!" is bravado you won't hear from many Kansas Citians. We let outsiders say that and more about our barbecue.

To paraphrase the late William Shawn, editor of the *New Yorker* magazine for many years: The more brilliant you are in your field, the less you'll brag about it. Shawn's wisdom doesn't resonate in today's barbecue culture, where blowing smoke about your pitmaster prowess and the superiority of your region's barbecue compared to other regions is the norm.

Missouri, a significant chunk of the bi-state Kansas/Missouri Kansas City metro area, is the "Show Me State." That slogan fits Kansas City–style barbecue: Why tell you how great it is when we can show you? The quality speaks for itself. Or, "No need to tell me. Show me!" The way to know Kansas City barbecue is to eat it.

This book leads barbecue lovers to the best places to eat great Kansas City barbecue. My job is to lead you there. Your job is to eat it. And just like the barbecue in Texas, Tennessee, and the Carolinas, you'll be wowed by some and not so impressed by others. Individual tastes, likes, and dislikes, vary. I'll tell you what I like, but I can't tell you what you like. As the old saw goes, "Concerning taste there is no argument." Or to borrow a concept from my friend, Stan Nelson, "The best barbecue is the barbecue you like!"

Kansas City pitmasters can blow smoke with the best of them. Our rich Midwestern/Southern culture, however, lands on the side of humility when it comes to bragging about our barbecue. We're proud of our barbecue. We let it speak for itself.

I love Kansas City barbecue. It's one of many reasons I live here. But you won't catch me saying that Kansas City barbecue is the best of the best, or that there's none better or as good as. Nope. I have savored barbecue from Austin, Lockhart, Luling, San Marcos, Lexington (North Carolina and Texas), Giddings, Memphis, Nashville, Lynchburg, Oklahoma City, Skiatook, Stillwater, Tulsa, Broken Arrow, Paducah, Charleston, Columbia (South Carolina and Missouri), Chapel Hill, Savannah, Decatur, Birmingham, St. Louis, Branson, Seattle, Madison, and many other communities that serve some of the best barbecue in America. You won't catch me throwing bones at Aaron Franklin's barbecue, or barbecue by Tootsie Tomanich, Smoky Jon Olson, Chris Lilly, Jack Cawthon, Nick Vergos, David Bessinger, Keith Allen, Ed Mitchell, or Flora Payne, to name a few.

Kansas City freely allows that our barbecue pitmasters stand on the shoulders of pitmasters, past and present, from Texas, Memphis, the Carolinas, Mississippi, Arkansas, Kentucky, and elsewhere. That's why our barbecue is so good. It is influenced by a diversity of sources from all over America and beyond.

On the other hand, we do not kiss the ring of barbecue pontiffs who represent their region as the world's greatest. They may allow that barbecue is available in other parts of the country, but they will have you thinking that barbecue in other regions is campfire-flamed roadkill compared to their "real" barbecue. Some accept beef, chicken, turkey, duck, lamb, and goat barbecue. Others cling to a long-held dogma that pork barbecue is the only real barbecue. I call it hogmatic hogwash, along with the dogma that the South is the birthplace of barbecue. Everybody knows that barbecue was a routine cooking method in Asia, Africa, Latin America, and Europe thousands of years before meat fires filled the air with barbecue smoke in North America. Thanks to our pitmasters, barbecue has become America's cuisine, but barbecue wasn't invented in America.

Kansas City barbecue has one foot in the past, the other in the present, starting to take the next step into the future. You'll savor the influence of both in the city that is globally famous for excellent barbecue. Let's get started.

What's a BBQ Lover?

Readers of this book fall into several categories, some of which overlap. One thing all share in common is a love of barbecue. Beyond that, there are Kansas City natives, Kansas Citians with backgrounds elsewhere, first-time visitors to Kansas City, occasional visitors to Kansas City, and frequent visitors to Kansas City.

Where a non-native or visitor comes from matters. Our origins and history are embedded in our palates. Some are able to judge Kansas City barbecue on its own merits. Others will measure it against the standards they have come to favor from their places of origin or other places they have frequented and loved.

Everyone who loves barbecue has opinions about what is good, bad, and best. More than a few Texans could have been the source of a famous cartoon by Kansas City's beloved cartoonist, the late Charles Barsotti, when he featured a forlorn bearded cowboy in a 10-gallon hat and Lone Star-studded cowboy boots, standing on a wooden deck next to a bullet smoker, an armadillo in the foreground. The caption was "How Kansas Citians can get really good bar-be-cue." How? The cowboy advises, "Take I-35 South to Lockhart,

Texas." Charlie loved Kansas City and his backyard barbecue, but he was true to his Texas roots.

There are good barbecue snobs and there are bad barbecue snobs. I count Barsotti among the good ones. Likewise, *Texas Monthly Barbecue* editor, Daniel Vaughn—a self-proclaimed barbecue snob—is a good one. Good ones have a sense of humor. They don't hold punches about what they think of the barbecue on the plate in front of them, but they aren't righteous, derogatory, or disrespectful. They are specific about what they like or don't like, but not in a pontifical, know-it-all tone.

Bad barbecue snobs are the opposite of good. At their worst, they are short on praise and long on criticism. They judge with a narcissistic posture. You don't learn much about barbecue from them, but you learn a lot about them if you care to pay attention. They are not strangers to boring and predictable.

Most barbecue lovers know what they like and don't like. They don't mind telling you what they like and don't like.

Some, especially those who are new to barbecue, haven't honed their personal sense of likes and dislikes. They are susceptible to the opinions of others—as if there's a Platonic objective standard for great barbecue, and they strive to understand it before they feel qualified to render their own opinions. Since there is so much variance in the quality of barbecue cooked by different pitmasters, the novice eventually learns that a Platonic standard doesn't exist. It comes down to what you as an individual like and don't like. You are the expert on that, and concerning what you like and don't like, there's no rebuttal. Others may not share your flavor preferences, but they can't deny them.

A Brief History of Kansas City Barbecue

Kansas City's Cowtown heritage set the stage for barbecue becoming the city's signature cuisine. Three elements essential to barbecue production on a massive scale converged in Kansas City in the early 1900s: abundant meat, hardwood, and pitmaster expertise.

A national rail, river ways, and highway transportation hub, the city was a natural attraction for workers seeking jobs in a growing agribusiness-fueled economy. Many early 20th-century newcomers were from the South. They brought their barbecue skills with them.

From their beginnings in the latter part of the 19th century, to the 1920s and '40s, Kansas City's stockyards and meat-processing plants were second only to Chicago's.

Tough or undesirable cuts such as ribs, brisket, snouts, ears, and feet did not go to waste, thanks to those who knew the barbecue method of cooking.

Barbecue as a product started on street corners. Using a variety of home-made cookers fashioned from steel drums and other improvised grills, week-end pitmasters smoked and sold barbecue that began to set a standard locals and visitors came to expect and count on.

Tennessee native Henry Perry, the Father of Kansas City Barbecue, sold barbecue pork, beef, opossum, woodchuck, and raccoon from his outdoor stand downtown as early as 1907. Later he moved into a building at 17th and Lydia. Arthur Bryant's Barbecue continues the Henry Perry legacy today. Anthony Rieke opened Rosedale Barbecue in 1934. It is the oldest continuously operating barbecue joint in Kansas City. Gates Bar-B-Q was established by George Gates in 1946. Russ Fiorella opened Smokestack Barbecue in 1957. It evolved into today's Jack Stack, founded by Russ' son, Jack Fiorella. At these and other early restaurants, workers learned the barbecue basics and went on to establish their own restaurants. Many Kansas City barbecue restaurants today were spawned from those early restaurants where the next generation of proprietors learned the art and business of barbecue.

Backyard barbecue enjoyed a surge of popularity in the 1930s in Kansas City and other cities, followed by a larger surge in suburban backyard barbecue in the 1950s.

By the late 1970s and early 1980s, barbecue as a sport emerged in the metro area, culminating in the founding of the Kansas City Barbeque Society in 1987.

What made it famous for barbecue? Most credit praise from visitors, sportscaster radio and TV banter, writers (especially Calvin Trillin), and celebrities—but most of all, the quality of the barbecue made Kansas City famous. The quality continues today, with a WOW! punch that resonates in your primal carnivore bones.

What is Kansas City Style?

Kansas City–style barbecue has changed over the past hundred years. In the old days meat went from the packing house or butcher shop to the pit, with little if any trimming. Today there is attention to presentation, especially since the 1980s when the contest scene emerged.

When Kansas City Barbeque Society (KCBS) contest rules and regulations were developed regarding appearance, tenderness, and taste, a new breed of Kansas City barbecue restaurants emerged: Contest-style. Neatly trimmed St. Louis cut ribs, membrane removed, sprinkled with dry rub, smoked until easily pulled from the bone, but not fall-off-the-bone, slathered or glazed with a sweet sauce and precisely sliced individual bones.

Typical meat specifications for Kansas City style

Brisket: neatly trimmed lean, scant traces of fat, moist, sliced thinner than in Texas, easy to pull apart, usually sauced unless requested naked in restaurants; up to cook in contests.

Pork shoulder: sliced, pulled, or chopped—tender and moist, sauced or not; cook's choice in contests; customer choice in restaurants, although some serve it sauced, no choice. A few places offer Carolina-style vinegar or mustard sauce with their pork.

Chicken: quarter, half or whole, is rubbed and smoked, juicy tender. Johnny's is crisped in a deep fryer bath before serving. Smoked or grilled chicken wings are also popular.

Turkey: moist, smoked breast and legs are most popular. Most breast meat is served thin-sliced; legs served whole.

Sausage: Kansas City doesn't have as many sausage makers as Texas, but we have enough variety to rival Texas, including hot links.

Lamb and mutton: available, smoked and sauced, but in only a few places.

Goat, cabrito: not a standard menu item in Kansas City barbecue restaurants.

Fish: smoked salmon and catfish available in select places; deep-fried catfish, halibut, cod on some menus, especially during spring Lenten season.

Duck (domestic or game), goose, venison, other game: not a standard menu item; can be custom-smoked, you supply the meat.

Other Kansas City menu items

There are other menu items that Kansas Citians expect to find in a barbecue joint. "You can't get by in Oklahoma without serving fried okra in your barbecue joint," Joe Davidson told me once at his Oklahoma Joe's restaurant in Broken Arrow, Oklahoma. Kansas City is another matter. Rarely will you find fried okra on a barbecue joint menu here. Kansas Citians really like potatoes, especially fries and potato salad. They are standard in most places, but a few get by with limiting their potato option to chips or cheesy potatoes. Here's the short list:

Beef brisket (thin sliced, compared to the thicker slices served in Texas)

Pork ribs (spares or babybacks; spares are dominant here instead of babybacks/loin ribs as in Memphis)

Burnt Ends

Chicken

Sausage

Rib tips

Beans

Coleslaw

Potatoes

Meat Quality

Along with the growth of competition barbecue—with cash prizes, fancy trophies and ribbons, and bragging rights for wins—came an increase in demand for high-quality meats. Instead of cheap, tough meats, teams went for, as one successful competitor remarked, "The best quality meat you can afford." That same practice carries over in barbecue restaurants, especially those with a competition pedigree.

When meat prices go up, restaurant owners and customers feel the pinch. Owners are faced with raising prices or reducing serving sizes. The only option with full or half slabs of ribs is to increase the price or make less money per slab. When the profit margin is slim already, most owners are forced to increase prices. This is a universal problem in the barbecue industry. A pitmaster/owner in Central Texas told me that he is seriously looking for alternative, less expensive meats. "Maybe I'll have to switch to armadillo," he remarked in jest.

Laboratory meat may be on the distant horizon, especially if production costs fall below the cost of traditional meat production and the savings are passed on to consumers. Consumer acceptance will be a crucial factor.

One word sums up Kansas City Style: eclectic.

The BBQ Joints

A Little BBQ Joint

1101 W 24 Hwy., Independence, MO 64050; (816) 252-2275; www.a littlebarbqjoint.com **Founded:** 2013 **Pitmaster:** Fabian Bauer **Wood:** Hickory

Fabian Bauer, former body man and gifted auto painter, is the perfect match to convert this building from a transmission repair shop to a barbecue emporium. Fabian's automotive artistry permeates this place outside and inside. Repurposed salvaged auto grills, hoods, trunk lids, lights, bumpers, spray guns, backseats, and small parts are put to work with a new purpose, functional or aesthetic.

Thanks to Fast Eddy Mauren, Fabian was a quick study in the art and science of smoked meat, churning out slow- and low-smoked barbecue meats from his Cookshack Fast Eddy pellet smoker. "Fast Eddy is my mentor," Fabian told me. Given Eddy's impeccable credentials as a champion pitmaster and barbecue pit designer, Fabian is in good hands. His line of barbecue cookers made by Cookshack out of Ponca City, Oklahoma, is becoming a familiar fixture in successful barbecue restaurants across the country.

It's a little barbecue joint for big appetites and an appreciation for the call of the road that future generations will look back on with astonishment. "You mean they drove those big machines under the control of one driver per car on two-lane roadways, speeding toward each other at 70 miles per hour or more!?"

Anyone who opens a barbecue restaurant in a city known as the Barbecue Capital of the World is a risk taker, especially if he has zero experience at working in a restaurant of any kind. Fabian didn't let that stop him. He built a little barbecue joint, and people came. So many came when he first opened the doors in April 2013 that he sold out the entire menu in a matter of hours. "Haven't you ever run a restaurant?" asked a disappointed prospective customer who showed up too late. "No," Fabian replied. He was too polite to say, "No, but I'm pretty darned happy that a barbecue newbie like me can open a little barbecue joint and get hammered with a sold out crowd like Aaron Franklin's in Austin on the very first day." He could have said that, but he didn't.

Like everyone else who succeeds in the barbecue business, Fabian stands on the shoulders of others. Besides Fast Eddy, Fabian's dad, Don Bauer, and daughter, Amy Bauer, help out every day. Fabian won't say whether his sauces are named after relatives or if the names speak of what you'll taste. Mean Mother-in-Law is his hottest sauce, followed by the Mad Housewife, which is sweet with a slightly fiery kick. Sweet Sister is his sweetest, mildest sauce.

Creative decor and language add fun at A Little BBQ Joint, but the barbecue is what brings you back. Fabian's ribs, sausage, pulled pork, brisket, and chicken are top-notch barbecue. If you only have room for one meat on your first visit, I highly recommend the burnt ends. Those cubed bites of barbecue brisket are melt-in-your mouth tender with a kiss of smoke. I don't let the Mean Mother-in-Law, Mad Housewife, or Sweet Sister get near my burnt ends, but if you want sauce, a tiny bit will complement.

Since A Little BBQ Joint is in Harry S Truman's hometown, Fabian put the "Harry S" on his menu to honor the American President. The Harry S is a grilled quarter-pound hot dog on a bun, topped with barbecue pulled pork and melted Jack cheese. It's a delicious tribute to Truman.

The sides complement the top quality of the barbecue. My friend Jay "The Snail" Vantuyl, who introduced me to this joint, always orders the hot—as in temperature, not seasonings—potato salad. It's a delicious bowl of warm chunks of boiled

Fresh Chicken

potatoes seasoned with herbs, spices, relish, and sauce that gives comfort to your palate. The fries, beans, slaw, and cheesy corn are likewise spark plug complements to the barbecue meat.

Kansas City is glad that the Bauer family and staff dared to position another barbecue joint in our competitive landscape. They take the risks, we get the benefits. Give them a try.

All Slabbed Up BBQ

405 Muncie Rd., Leavenworth, KS 66048; (913) 727-5227; No website
Founded: 2007 **Pitmaster:** Charlie Browne **Wood:** Oak & hickory
Leavenworth is known for its prisons: a federal penitentiary, a military prison on the grounds of Fort Leavenworth, and a state penitentiary in the neighboring city of Lansing. No wonder the nearby distillery brand is "Most Wanted." (It isn't like the hooch inmates make in prison.) Likewise, the Slabbed Up cuisine is superior to slammer cuisine.

Charlie Browne owns All Slabbed Up. Unlike the other Charlie, whose efforts fall short of perfection, the Charlie of All Slabbed Up is succeeding. Charlie Browne is not as well-known as the other Charlie, but he is earning the praise of thousands of fans for his barbecue.

All Slabbed Up's tomato base sauce with a smoky vinegar/molasses accent pairs well with the barbecue meats: ribs, brisket, burnt ends, pork, ham,

sausage, and turkey. It's all good. My favorite is a beef and rib combo with
fresh-cut, skin-on fries mixed with fried onions and the sweet-sauce barbecue
pit beans. The hot cheesy potato salad, sweet potato fries, and fried pickles are
also stand-outs.

All Slabbed Up is small, with wooden floors, western memorabilia on the
walls, and galvanized steel roofing on the ceiling and wrapped around the bar.
You get the feeling that love of country, love of girlfriends and Mama, trains,
pickups, whiskey, and longnecks, mixed with love pains, loss pains, blame, and
all of that drama dear to our country-music-loving hearts is no stranger at All
Slabbed Up. There's a strong John Wayne presence as well. If a plate of All
Slabbed Up barbecue with sides and a cold brew doesn't cheer you up, it's time
to see a therapist.

Arthur Bryant's

1727 Brooklyn Ave., Kansas City, MO 64127; (816) 231-1123; second
location at Legends at the Kansas Speedway, 1702 Village West
Pkwy., Kansas City, KS 66111; (913) 788-7500; www.arthurbryantsbbq
.com **Founded:** 1908 by Henry Perry, then Charlie Bryant, then
Arthur Bryant. **Pitmaster:** Timmy Brown **Wood:** Oak & hickory

> "This is a personal business. I have to know what is going on. If I don't
> it's too bad.
>
> I don't hire me a barbecue man to come in here and do it. I'm the
> barbecue man."
>
> > Arthur Bryant, as quoted in *The Kansas City Star*,
> > December 28, 1982

Arthur Bryant's can rightly claim to be the restaurant that is most responsi-
ble for making Kansas City famous for barbecue. Sportscasters from the old
nearby baseball stadium exclaimed over the inviting aroma of meat fires wafting from Bryant's barbecue pit. And when they raved about the quality of the
smoked meat and grainy vinegar base sauce that they soon acquired a taste
for, who could not want to come to Kansas City for barbecue?

Later, when native son turned New York writer, humorist, and culinary
adventurer, Calvin Trillin, extolled the wonders of free burnt end scraps you
could reach in from the serving line and help yourself to, plus the plates of
smoked meats and freshly cut lard-fried fries, it sealed the deal. Especially
after Trillin proclaimed Bryant's to be the single best restaurant in the world.

Mr. Bryant took the fame and hyperbole with humility, often remarking
that, "It's just a grease house."

Grease house or not, even after the city mourned Mr. Bryant's passing
in late December 1982, Arthur Bryant's on Brooklyn Avenue remains a holy
place, the esteemed grease house palace of Kansas City barbecue.

Some days you'll be lucky and the serving line will be short. Other days
the line will be out the door. When the line is long and you have time to wait 45
minutes to an hour to be served, be patient and wait. Think of it as your way to
pay homage to one of Kansas City's "barbecue man" legends.

Your beef order will be lean and tender or marbled with flavorful fat. You
won't be asked if you want it marbled or lean. You get what the server grabs.

The ribs vary from tender, meaty, and juicy to flavorful but on the dry side,
depending upon how long they've been waiting for you in the pit. All of Bryant's meats have a just-right kiss of oak smoke.

On your first visit I recommend saying "beef and fries" when you hand your plate to the counterman after he says, "Next," or "What'll you have?" Mr. Bryant's roots were in Texas, beef brisket country. Brisket is what he knew and what he did best. Beef and fries is the signature plate at Arthur Bryant's.

Mr. Bryant's original sauce is so different from what most people think of as barbecue sauce that the sour, grainy vinegar base liquid with hints of curry, cumin, cayenne, and pit drippings won't have you exclaiming, "Wow! This is fantastic!" at first taste. Give it some time and you could acquire a taste for it, as I did only a few hours after my first visit. I was glad I bought a bottle to satisfy my craving for a midnight snack of leftover beef with sauce.

I'm not saying you shouldn't try the pulled pork or burnt ends on the menu—fairly recent additions—but be advised that they are tossed in a sweet sauce and aren't available without sauce. The burnt ends, like most of what you get in restaurants today due to massive popularity, are cubes of brisket instead of the brisket trimmings from the old days. The pulled pork, likewise, is sauced and may not resonate with Carolina palates.

Fries are mandatory. Vegans: be advised that Bryant's fries are cooked in extremely hot lard, imparting a sweetness that can only be imitated with New York duck fat.

Thanks to Gary Berbiglia, former co-owner after Mr. Bryant's death, two new sauces were added to the Bryant's lineup: Sweet Heat and Rich and Spicy. Both are less grainy than the original and add a touch of sweetness to the mix. Sweet Heat, with its tingle of fire, has become a favorite of mine. Gary can also be credited with formulating the Original to Mr. Bryant's standards. Mr. Bryant didn't leave a recipe behind, just a list of ingredients without proportions. Gary nailed it after several tries.

Asado Urban Grill

Hilton – Kansas City Airport, 8801 NW 112th St., Kansas City, MO 64153; (816) 891-8911; www3.hilton.com/en/hotels/missouri/hilton-kansas-city-airport-MCIAPHF/dining/index.html **Founded:** 2014 **Pitmaster:** Zachary Alft **Wood:** Hickory & cherry

"Where's Café Weatherby? Where's Chef Rob? Can we still eat barbecue here?"

Most fans of Chef Rob Magee, former Café Weatherby executive chef at the Airport Hilton, know that Rob is now executive chef, co-owner, and head pitmaster at the new virally popular Q39 in midtown Kansas City. The space formerly known as Café Weatherby is Asado Urban Grill, with a new look, new menu, and new executive chef, Zachary Alft.

Although there's no doubt that Asado is in a hotel and conference center, the restaurant has its own style and feel that imparts a welcoming, relaxed atmosphere: gray walls, subdued lighting, and glass panels lit from behind with an orange hue, each featuring spices, herbs, and other food preparation basics.

In Spain, Brazil, Argentina, and Uruguay, *asado* means charcoal grilled or roasted meat, or a gathering of people to eat asado. Traditional asado fare, such as suckling pigs, sausages, flank steaks, and grilled vegetables, are not on the Asado Urban Grill menu. Since Asado's urban context is Kansas City, where visitors expect Kansas City–style barbecue, Chef Alft accommodates that expectation with smoked chicken soup, smoked burgers, grilled chicken, and smoked brisket sandwiches, available for lunch or dinner. Treat yourself to Asado's fries and the house-made potato chips with your sandwich. Order both. I like to dip them in barbecue sauce.

The "After Five" menu features additional barbecue options: smoked pork spareribs, smoked chicken, smoked brisket platter, grilled beef tenderloin, grilled ribeye steak, grilled KC strip loin steak, and grilled Colorado lamb chops. Chef Alft uses hickory and cherry to smoke Asado meats in the Hilton's Southern Pride woodburning barbecue pit and smoker. After Five sides include au gratin potatoes, fries, baked beans, and a vegetable of the day.

Chef Alft's local suppliers include Farm to Market Bakery, Local Pig, and Scavuzzo's Food Service.

Asado's barbecue is tender, juicy, and not overpowered with too much smoke or seasonings, which should satisfy the taste buds of almost everyone. The tomato base barbecue sauce fuses Kansas City's two sauce traditions—sour and sweet—with perfect balance and no fiery or unusual seasonings to distract your palate from the natural flavors of the meat. If Asado is a visitor's first taste of Kansas City–style barbecue, they will find this to be a great introduction.

B.B.'s Lawnside Blues & BBQ

1205 E 85th St., Kansas City, MO 64131; (816) 822-7427; bbslawside bbq.com **Founded:** 1990 **Pitmaster:** Mike Nickle **Wood:** Hickory

Barbecue doesn't get more "Kansas City style" than at B.B.'s. It's a roadside shack that survived Prohibition to later become the greatest live blues and barbecue emporium north and west of the Mississippi Delta. Co-owners Lindsay and Jo Shannon have made B.B.'s Kansas City's major go-to place for barbecue, blues, and good times.

B.B.'s barbecue pit is made from granite pavers that did former duty at crosswalks when most Kansas City streets were dirt that turned to mud from rainstorms and melted snow. And there's more blues shaking B.B.'s walls in a month than in all Kansas City barbecue joints combined for a hundred years and counting. This is where the blues and barbecue are on a first-name basis. The regulars know and love them both.

B.B.'s is as close as you can get to the Mississippi Delta blues and barbecue tradition, with a distinct Kansas City accent. The barbecue is Kansas City style. Some of the sides are Louisiana style: Smokey Jo's Gumbo, Swamp Man Boudin Balls, Louisiana Goulash, Red Beans & Rice, Dirty Red's Jambalaya, and a Cajun Wrap. The only thing missing is tamales. For that you'll have to go to the Hot Tamale Trail in the Delta—or get B.B.'s carryout, add some tamales from a local Mexican restaurant or bodega, crank up a blues album, pop some ice cold Dixie longnecks, and party down!

I'm a longtime fan of B.B.'s beans, and would make a meal of a big helping were it not for the other good stuff on the menu. I also love the barbecue feast in a Mason jar, B.B.'s Barbecue Sundae: a layer of barbecue beans topped with coleslaw and a final overflowing topping of pulled pork, with a pickle spear garnish. Yum! When you're in the mood for fish, try B.B.'s Memphis Minnie's Smoked Catfish. You'll find the recipe in this book, but nothing beats eating it on location. B.B.'s of course has all of the barbecue meats you expect in a Kansas City barbecue restaurant: ribs, rib tips, pulled pork, brisket, turkey, and sausage—all hickory smoked in B.B.'s historic pit.

Mike Nickle, B.B.'s stellar pitmaster, started at B.B.'s at age 18. He quickly moved from bussing tables and other duties to tending the pit. Mike and his brother Jimmy, front of the house manager at B.B.'s, cook together on a competition barbecue team. You can't get more passionate about barbecue than making a living at it and competing at barbecue contests in your free time. You'll appreciate the results of that passion when you eat B.B.'s barbecue.

Lindsay is a blues expert and aficionado extraordinaire. He knows the musicians, the singer/songwriters, the context, the histories, and the cultural significance of the blues in American culture. In addition to Lindsay and Jo's exemplary blues and barbecue emporium, Lindsay hosts a popular Sunday night Kansas City Blues Show on KCFX 101 The Fox. The show is still going strong after almost three decades on the air.

Bates City Bar B Que

6493 Quivera Rd., Shawnee, KS 66216; (913) 962-7447; www.batescity bbq.net **Founded:** 2000 **Pitmaster:** Tom Roberts **Wood:** Hickory

Bates City is full of eye candy: a mix of Kansas City Chiefs and Royals memorabilia, player photos, posters, and vast expanses covered with used license vanity barbecue license plates and number plates, like GOTRIBS, MAGIC, and so forth. It's a wonder that the building doesn't sink under the weight of all that metal.

Although Bates City Bar B Que has been at home in Shawnee, Kansas, for more than two decades, the only way you'll likely hear about it is from friends or fans who happen to mention it. I haven't found any place else in town that has maintained a consistently low price for a slab of spareribs. If more people knew about it, the line would be out the door every lunch and dinner hour.

On the spectrum of competition rib quality—appearance, tenderness, and taste—the low-cost slab of Bates City ribs would not muster high marks on appearance and tenderness. The slab is traditional Kansas City style, untrimmed and unskinned. You get the whole slab, with breast bone and brisket flap that contest cooks trim off St. Louis style. The slab is cut so you can grab one rib at a time, but don't expect neat, precisely cut ribs. These bone side up ribs are cut fast and functional with a cleaver or chef's knife. And if you hold to the contest judging standard that takes points off for fall-off-the-bone ribs, go ahead and mark them down on your imaginary score card, but don't stop short of taking a bite. Judges may be trained to say they are "overcooked," but I'm in the camp that says they are cooked to perfection. Mushy ribs are where I draw the line on "overcooked." Bates City ribs are not mushy.

Bates City also serves some of the best fries in town: hand-cut fresh in house and deep-fried, crispy on the outside and so tasty. Likewise their

made-from-scratch coleslaw gets high marks: simple dressing with a touch of sugar; nothing fancy, but really good.

Tom Roberts, Bates City owner/pitmaster, and his good friend Mike Atwood in Bates City, decided to go into the barbecue business in 1976. Mike owns and operates the original Bates City barbecue in Bates City, Missouri. Roberts opened Bates City Bar B Que in Shawnee in 2000, one of the best barbecue joints in town for price and quality.

The BBQ Shack

1613 E Peoria St., Paola, KS 66071; (913) 294-5908; www.thebbqshack .com **Founded:** 2006 **Pitmaster:** Rick Schoenberger **Wood:** Hickory

"I like this place and willingly could waste my time in it."
- (Act II, Scene IV)
"Can one desire too much of a good thing?"
- (Act IV, Scene I)
William Shakespeare, *As You Like It*

Rick Schoenberger, also known as "Shake," can only guess as to why his dad's co-workers at the Delco Battery Plant in Olathe nicknamed him Shakespeare. Was it his hairline resembling images of the late playwright and poet, William Shakespeare? Did it allude to fishing with Shakespeare® rods and reels? He has asked his dad, and he doesn't know either.

Rick only knows that some of the nicknames were transferred to the children of the Delco workers by their peers from grade school forward. Although

Shake doesn't get absorbed in reading Shakespeare plays or sonnets during his rare moments of free time, he is known as a big fan of another drama series, *The Andy Griffith Show* and *Mayberry R.F.D.*

If you're an Andy fan you'll be in your element when you step inside The BBQ Shack. If you're a fan of great barbecue and sides, you'll also be in your element. If you're neither, you could be both by the time you dine and leave. The BBQ Shack has a mix of humor, eye candy, friendly service, excellent barbecue, and great sides that is sure to please.

Shake's menu is loaded with barbecue delights, most named after or alluding to characters or places in Mayberry R.F.D. Don't miss the Checkpoint Chicky Wings, followed by a sampling of superb barbecue meats like pork ribs, beef brisket, pork, turkey, ham, sausage, chicken, and fantastic sides. Pick some combo options, take home the leftovers, and plan some return visits to graze through the entire menu.

As you scan the fun decor, don't miss John the deer. Shake's creative humor is evident throughout this fun place—and his pitmaster talents are to barbecue what the bard's talents were to sonnets and plays. The BBQ Shack is indeed a good thing.

Bee Cee's Authentic Bar-B-Que

12560 Quivera Rd., Overland Park, KS 66213; (913) 897-4500; www .beeceesauthenticbbq.com **Founded:** 2002 (at current location since 2013) **Pitmaster:** Craig Nelson **Wood:** Hickory

Native Kansas Citian Craig Nelson, pitmaster/owner at Bee Cee's, brings a combination of backyard smokology and learning from the pros to his Bee Cee's barbecue establishment. Before taking the leap into the Kansas City barbecue restaurant scene, he learned the dos, don'ts, and other pit dynamics of the barbecue business from Dr. Rich Davis and staff at the former KC Masterpiece Barbecue Restaurant and at Fiorella's Jack Stack. That's a respectable pedigree for any pitmaster, and you can tell by the menu and the quality of the barbecue at Bee Cee's that Craig paid attention. He learned well and developed his own "Simply Divine" signature flavor that any regular at Bee Cee's can instantly recognize at a blind tasting: "That's Bee Cee's." Two qualities give instant recognition: Bee Cee's barbecue—be it the ribs, the rib tips, the chicken, the wings, sausage, pork, beef, or burnt ends—is tender and smoky. Craig uses his own dry seasonings on the meat, cooks it slow and low with 100 percent hickory smoke in an electric smoker, and slathers a moderate amount of his sweet secret blend smooth tomato base barbecue sauce on it unless you request it naked with sauce on the side. Either way, you're in for a treat.

If you're concerned about the wings being dry, as in some joints: not to worry. Craig has mastered the art of smoking Bee Cee's jumbo wings to the same level of tenderness as his other meats. You can get them regular or Cajun hot. Save room for a side of fries, beans, potato salad, or slaw.

Bee Cee's opened in 2001. Craig and his son, the late Bradford Cornelius "Bee Cee" Nelson moved the restaurant from Kansas City, Missouri, to the current location, a gas station/convenience store near the Johnson County Community College and Kansas University Edwards campuses, in 2013.

Biemer's BBQ

2120 W Ninth St., Lawrence, KS 66049; (785) 842-0800; www.biemers. com **Founded:** 2008 **Pitmaster:** Jim Biemick **Wood:** Oak, apple, cherry, pecan

Jim Biemick has been churning out mouthwatering barbecue for University of Kansas students, KU Jayhawk fans, and metro Kansas Citians since opening Biemer's BBQ in this former hamburger joint in 2008. When you walk in, you can tell by the aromas, friendly staff, and abundance of pig art that you're in a barbecue joint and you're going to like this place.

Jim was raised in southern Illinois in an area known for apples, apple-wood, and great barbecue. After a career as a golf pro in Chicago, he settled in various states, selling golf equipment for Spalding Top-Flite.

Minute Maid
Sprite
Coca-Cola
WE RUB
OUR MEAT
DAILY.
BIEMER'S BBQ
LAWRENCE, KANSAS

Be glad that Jim brought his barbecue skills and passion for barbecue with him when he settled in Lawrence. Biemer's is one of Lawrence's favorite spots for pulled pork, beef brisket, smoked turkey, sausage, ribs, and chicken wings, smoked in an Ole Hickory smoker with oak, apple, cherry, and sometimes pecan.

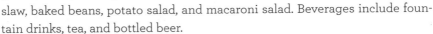

Sides include baked potato, fries, onion rings, sweet tots, fried green beans, fried pickles, coleslaw, baked beans, potato salad, and macaroni salad. Beverages include fountain drinks, tea, and bottled beer.

Biemer's barbecue meat is cooked fresh each day. Although sauce is available, Biemer's is so proud of the barbecue that their slogan is "Meat this good don't need no sauce!" If you want sauce, there are four styles to suit your taste: original traditional tomato base, sweet and tangy, vinegar, and hot vinegar.

Jim is a self-taught pitmaster, but you can tell that he learned a lot early on during his years in Illinois. When he decided to reinvent himself as a professional barbecue pitmaster, he did a lot of experimenting, cooking in contests, and getting various tips from other pitmasters. He bought a portable rig and sold barbecue at car shows and motorcycle shows. Before opening the restaurant at the current location, he sold barbecue out of a Phillips 66 station. Biemer's many fans in Lawrence and metro Kansas City hope he stays right where he is, continuing to smoke barbecue so good it "don't need no sauce!"

Big Q Barbecue

2117 S 34th St., Kansas City, KS 66106; (913) 362-6980; **Pitmasters:** Rusty Quick & Gary Wright **Wood:** Hickory

Big Q is not a secret. Many Kansas Citians haven't heard of it because it's on Maple Hill in Kansas City, Kansas, off the beaten path. Folks in the know haven't deliberately kept it a secret. You didn't ask.

Although Big Q's fan base is large, you wouldn't know it unless you're there during an especially busy lunch or dinner hour. A diverse swath of humanity stops by to dine-in or carry out daily. Customers arrive solo, in couples, and in groups. They are construction workers, road repair crews, soldiers, law enforcement officers, elected officials, business executives, office workers, busy moms and dads stopping between errands, and first-timers who found Big Q en route from KCI. They like the 100 percent hickory pit meat that Rusty and Gary excel at smoking to juicy flavorful perfection. They like the price/ quantity value. They like the spicy red sauce. They like the friendly service and the opportunity to get to know the pitmasters/owners. Rusty Quick and Gary Wright have greeted and fed their loyal customers with the help of Big Q's friendly, efficient staff, for 30 years in the same location.

Don't expect fancy appointments at Big Q. It is not a white tablecloth, wood beams, brick and high ceiling kind of place. Its freestanding building could be mistaken for a hamburger emporium at first glance, due to the glassed-in sunroom—a barbecue joint

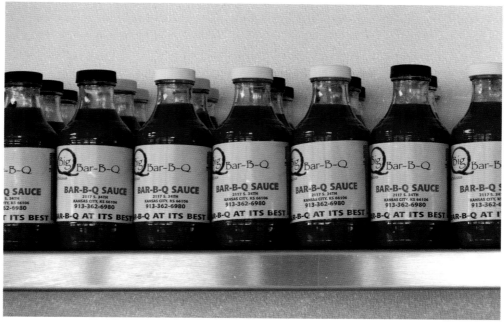

rarity. Rusty Quick and Gary Wright designed the building with the barbecue pit far enough back from the sunroom glass to avoid clouding the view with smoke residue.

Rusty and Gary proudly stand with the old school of Kansas City pitmasters. They barbecue in Big Q's original brick pit, fueled with 100 percent hickory. True to the Anthony Rieke method that the Quick family learned at Rosedale, Rusty and Gary hang their untrimmed, unskinned pork slabs in a brick pit fueled with flaming, smoking hickory logs. The ribs, along with other meats on grill racks, smoke slow and low to a juicy tenderness loaded with natural umami.

Rusty and Gary get top honors for all of their barbecue, especially their ribs and brisket. Add beans, fries, coleslaw, and Big Q's signature onion rings. I wouldn't throw bones at any of Big Q's barbecue, but I'm especially partial to the beef, ribs, beans, and fries combo. I prefer naked barbecue with a pool of sauce on the side for dipping. It is no problem if I forget to ask for sauce on the side at Biq Q. Rusty and Gary don't drown their barbecue in sauce. There's a squeeze bottle of sauce and catsup on each table if you want more.

The good old standby national brand beers are available, plus Corona, but until Maple Hill gets its own microbrewery, I enjoy the feast with ice water or tea.

Quick is a longtime distinguished name in Kansas City barbecue history, where it stands for slow-smoked barbecue, nothing resembling fast food. Rusty and Gary started the business as a way to provide for their families and put the kids through school. Those goals are accomplished. Now it's apparent that the other driving force all along has been their love of barbecue. The kids are through school, but Rusty and Gary aren't ready to quit after more than 30 years. They agree that running Big Q "is a labor of love."

Love and barbecue were never meant to be a big secret on Maple Hill. When you're anywhere near, by chance or by choice, stop by for some Big Q barbecue.

Big T's Barbecue

6201 Blue Pkwy., Kansas City, MO 64129; (816) 923-2278; second location at 9409 Blue Ridge Blvd., Kansas City, MO 64138; (816) 767-0905; www.letseat.at/bigtsbarbq **Founded:** 1970s as Oscar's BBQ; changed name to Big T's in 1992 **Pitmaster:** Timothy Jones **Wood:** Hickory

"We're Smokin' It Right!"

The family owned flagship Big T's on Blue Parkway is within sight of LC's Bar-B-Q on Blue Parkway. Bring a hearty appetite and pace yourself to graze at

both. A long, stainless steel–topped order/pickup counter with a large menu board posted above and behind it awaits your action when you step inside. Also behind the counter is a kitchen/prep area and a brick pit with heavy steel doors that is a work of barbecue art to the faithful. A few dining tables and chairs sit against the wall.

To your right as you face the counter is the main dining room. The wood planked floor shows well-worn character. The booths and tables are showing wear, but are comfortable. Old farming implements are displayed on some of the walls, along with a large full-color mural depicting two mules pulling a sod-busting plow guided by a farmer in a straw hat. Trees, chickens, cattle, pigs, a weathered home, and a red barn in the background complete the scene.

Framed sports posters and news reprints provide historical glimpses. One is headlined, "420 Feet is 420 Feet No Matter What Color Your Skin Is." There's also an enlarged, framed old ad for Oscar's Bar-B-Q with the same address as Big T's Blue Parkway location, with the street designated as East 50 Highway. "We may not sell the most in town, but we sell the best anywhere around," touts the ad, followed by, "Barbecue Headquarters for the K.C. Royals."

Oscar Jones started this place in the 1970s and called it his own until his son Timothy was born. Oscar changed the name to Big T's in honor of Tim in 1992. Now Tim runs both Big T's restaurants, the original and the Blue Ridge Boulevard location that opened in 2007. When Oscar isn't enjoying his favorite hobby, fishing, he stops in for a quality control assessment.

Royals and Chiefs fans know Big T's. It's an easy on/off I-435 to the stadium complex. A lucky

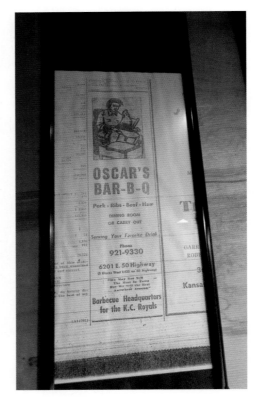

few who reserve a rental grill for tailgating have an easy pick-up and return. Others prefer to pick up game-day hickory smoked barbecue that's fresh from Big T's pit. Kansas City baseball legend, the beloved Buck O'Neil, was a Big T's fan. B.B. King and many Kansas City Chiefs and Royals players have chowed down on Big T's barbecue.

Big T's menu is a medley of Kansas City favorites along with a couple of items—greens, corn on the cob, beef hot links, and beef ribs—that aren't widely available in Kansas City barbecue joints. Beef ribs are sold on weekends only. My favorite is a combo double-decker sandwich with sliced beef and sliced pork with fries and beans, or a beef burnt ends open face with fries and beans. Order your meat dry, with sauce on the side so you can dip or pour as much sauce as you wish. Every menu item has its fans. Rib tips are the best seller. Graze your way through the menu on multiple occasions and pick your own favorites.

TAILGATING
KANSAS CITY STYLE

Tailgating happens in a variety of venues, but the major action in Kansas City is on home game days for the Chiefs or Royals. Kansas City tailgaters are passionate about their barbecue, their sides, and our Kansas City Chiefs and Royals. Some say Kansas City has raised the bar for excellence in tailgating and that it is unequaled anywhere else. It's like the difference between burning a bratwurst on a grill versus smoking a slab of ribs to perfection. Others within the professional football leagues would heartily disagree. Does it really matter who is best as long as there's good food and good times, friendly rivalry, and some brews in moderation? Before you decide to join the fun, talk with experienced tailgaters for advice, and go online for ideas and tips.

Big' Uns Grill – Wood Smoked & Charcoal Grilled Meats

1620 SW Sixth St., Topeka, KS 66606; (785) 861-7259; www.bigunsgrill.com
Founded: 2013 **Pitmaster:** Lee Atwood
Wood: Hickory

Brothers Lee and Craig Atwood have only been in the barbecue business in Topeka since 2013, but they know smoke, and their passion for barbecue excellence has already put them on the KC Metro barbecue map. They are stick burners in the Central Texas tradition, cooking in Lee's hand-built pit, fashioned from a 500-gallon propane tank with a fire box on the side and a reverse flow chimney. They smoke or grill all meats on the menu, and all of their sides are homemade fresh. Bring a big appetite and try a combo with ribs, burnt ends, pulled pork, beans, and fries. Or if you're feeling seriously decadent, try the Heart Attack Fries topped with melted cheese and chopped barbecue meats. The inside is functional and comfortable, not fancy. The barbecue will not disappoint.

Bigg's BBQ Grill & Bar

2429 Iowa St., Lawrence, KS 66046; (785) 856-2550; www.biggsribs
.com **Founded:** 2004 **Pitmaster:** Doug Holiday **Wood:** Hickory

Bigg's flagship restaurant on Iowa Street in Lawrence is a popular hangout for university crowds and sports bar fans. The interior features subdued lighting, old fashioned tin ceilings, and wooden floors. The walls are covered with '60s and '70s rock memorabilia, including framed *Rolling Stone* magazine covers featuring Pink Floyd, Nirvana, Grateful Dead, and others, tinted by transitions of pink, blue, and green lighting reflected from the ceiling.

TVs are scattered throughout so fans can watch in-season sports while chowing down on Bigg's lightly sauced hickory smoked babyback ribs, brisket, pulled pork, spareribs, chicken, ham, burnt ends, and hot link sausage. This

being a sports bar in a university town, there's also a popular burger on the menu, the Jay Hog, two quarter-pound beef patties topped with cheese and strips of smoked bacon with a bacon-dijonnaise condiment. My favorites at Bigg's are the burnt ends, babyback ribs, and pit beans, but every item on the menu has its fans. Three excellent Bigg's sauces are served on the side with each order.

Owner/Operator Doug Holiday and his wife, Shawn, also own Burgers by Bigg's and Bigg's on Mass in Lawrence.

Boss Hawg's Barbeque

2833 SW 29th St., Topeka, KS 66614; (785) 273-7300; http://boss hawgsbbq.com **Founded:** 1986 **Pitmaster:** Ben Platte **Wood:** Hickory & oak

What's a lady to do? She bought a legendary barbecue joint in a city that's better known for blowing political smoke than for its barbecue smoke. Thanks to Boss Hawg's founders, Elizabeth and the late Hank Lumpkin, the smoke from SW 29th Street is more famous than the smoke that blows from the capitol dome in downtown Topeka.

Just like Elizabeth, Sarah Burtch, the new owner of Boss Hawg's, knows smoke, and she knows how to carry on Hank and Elizabeth Lumpkin's legacy of great barbecue in the capital city of Kansas.

Boss Hawg's started as a catering and carryout business. As contest awards and customer demand escalated, Hank and Elizabeth decided to take the leap and go into the barbecue restaurant business. Thanks to their pitmaster/business/marketing skills, it worked! Boss Hawg's was established as the go-to place for great barbecue in Topeka. Hank and Elizabeth worked overtime to keep up with demand. It got the best of Hank. He died of heart failure at the restaurant on August 19, 2003, at 38 years old. It was a very sad day for the barbecue

community. Elizabeth kept Boss Hawg's going for several years after Hank's death, eventually selling the entire operation—the restaurant and Pig Skin's Bar—in 2013 to Sarah Burtch. Sarah has channeled the strengths of Hank and Elizabeth, along with her own talents, to make Boss Hawg's a happening place of barbecue excellence in Topeka and the state of Kansas.

Brobecks Barbeque

4615 Indian Creek Pkwy. (106th & Roe), Overland Park, KS 66207; (913) 901-9700; www.brobecksbbq.com **Founded:** 2007 **Pitmaster:** Doug Brobeck, with sons Dean & Dave **Wood:** Hickory

A prominent sign hangs from the ceiling near the cash register: "Welcome to Brobecks BBQ. The only BBQ in KC where you can bring your own sauce." I respect a place that dares to invite you to bring your own sauce. Besides their own house sauces, Doug Brobeck, owner/pitmaster, also has some Kansas City favorites on hand for customers, Gates and KC Masterpiece among them. Brobeck knows that good barbecue is about the meat. Sauce is a complement, not the main course.

You can start a sauce versus meat argument in Kansas City, Memphis, Austin, or any other place where the barbecue faithful are gathered. Some say anyone can barbecue meat: it's the sauce that makes the difference. Others say the best barbecue needs no sauce.

It needn't be either/or, although I beg to differ with those who say anyone can barbecue meat. Were that true, all barbecue would be tender, never tough, and kissed with smoke instead of having no smoke flavor at all or being so smoky that the meat flavor is bitter.

My advice has always been to use sauce in moderation. If the sauce doesn't complement the flavor of the meat, don't use it. There are many sauces, homemade and commercially available, that do a great job of complementing barbecue meat.

I tried the beef brisket, pork ribs, and sausage with and without sauce. They are tender, with a lingering kiss of smoke without sauce, although you

can do no harm with a touch of Brobecks tomato base/molasses sauce or a touch of KC Masterpiece Original.

Brobecks house-made Carolina-style mustard sauce is especially good with the pulled pork sandwich. I also like to dip my fries in a puddle of mustard sauce.

When our server brought a sample of Brobecks ham salad, I thought, "Oh no. This is going to taste like the ham salad Aunt Minnie used to bring to the annual Hamm family reunion in Stillwater, Oklahoma, years ago." I changed her name to protect the guilty. I never cared for Aunt Minnie's ham salad.

Brobecks ham salad is nothing like Aunt Minnie's. The combination of smoked ham, smoked turkey, relish, and other seasonings make this salad good enough to be your entree.

Brobecks fries, crispy outside/melt-in-your-mouth inside, with fresh, not greasy, flavor, are some of the best in Kansas City, as are the extra-cheesy corn nuggets.

Doug Brobeck brought his East Tennessee/Appalachian Mountains barbecue expertise and palate to town and adapted his style to Kansas City tastes. We're glad he did.

Burnt End BBQ

11831 Metcalf Ave., Overland Park, KS 66210; (913) 451-8888; www .burntendbbqkc.com **Founded:** 2011 **Pitmaster:** Stephen "Smokey" Schwartz **Wood:** Hickory

Kansas City's PB&J Restaurant group has a reputation for operating quality restaurants with good food and good service. They make good on that reputation with Burnt End BBQ.

It's a new freestanding building in a southern Johnson County shopping center, where I didn't expect to find good barbecue.

A savvy feature at Burnt End BBQ is their bowl options. You can get a variety of meat options with your choice of two sides and a generous slice of cornbread—all gluten-free. Smart move, given the increasing demand for gluten-free menu options. If you want a couple of slices of bread to make a meat sandwich, ask for it when you order and they will oblige.

I'm a fan of fried pickles, especially dill pickle chips in batter. I prefer that they be made from scratch on the premises instead of generic from a restaurant supply vendor. Burnt End makes some of the best I've ever eaten.

If you like fried pickles, don't pass them up when they are available as an appetizer special. Beer battered, with jalapeño aioli, ranch, and barbecue sauce dips, these chips work well as an appetizer or a complementary side dish with any sandwich or entree.

Sauce choices are Original, Traditional Thick 'n' Bold, Honey Blaze, Sweet Chipotle BBQ Blaze, and Spicy Southwest.

Pitmaster Stephen "Smokey" Schwartz has been involved in Kansas City barbecue since 1982, when he and some friends opened the former Joe's Barbecue affiliated with Joe's Barn in Olathe.

Later he worked the pits as executive chef and pitmaster at Chow Town's legendary Fiorella's Jack Stack for more than 10 years before joining the PB&J team in 2005. Smokey has competed against other chefs in venues such as a Share our Strength fundraiser in Chicago, where his Burnt End Bowl won a battle of the chef's competition against stellar chefs from other cities. Smokey has won that competition an unprecedented three times! He also competes at the Great Lenexa BBQ Battle with the PB&J Smokin' Old Men team.

Burnt End offers a complete menu of the meats you expect in a barbecue restaurant, but the bowls are what attracted my attention. The signature Burnt End Bowl features burnt ends, pit beans, cornbread, and onion straws. Other options include the pulled pork Pig Out Bowl; the brisket, ham, bacon, cheddar Jack cheese, fried potatoes and onion straws 119th Street Bowl; or a bowl of your choice of two meats, two sides, and cornbread. I chose the latter, with a combo of burnt ends, pulled pork, pit beans, and cheesy corn, with add-on servings of coleslaw and beer-battered fried dill pickle chips. It was so good that I called it barbecue bliss in a bowl. The burnt ends were tender and flavorful with a kiss of smoke; likewise the pulled pork with a slightly sweet tomato base sauce. Smokey clearly believes in using enough seasoning to enhance, not overpower, the natural meat flavors. He also strives to keep it local as much as possible with his meat and produce suppliers.

Balanced seasonings, real barbecue with a creative twist, and a talented pitmaster make Burnt End a winner on the Kansas City barbecue scene.

Char Bar Smoked Meats & Amusements

4050 Pennsylvania Ave., Kansas City, MO 64111; (816) 389-8600; http://charbarkc.com **Founded:** 2014 **Pitmaster:** Mitch Benjamin **Wood:** Hican

Char Bar ended a barbecue drought in Westport with a menu that appeals to Kansas City's hardcore barbecue lovers and growing numbers of vegetarians.

All are welcome at Char Bar, where competition-style barbecue shares the table with gourmet Southern-style sides. Some of the sides are hearty enough to satisfy carnivores, omnivores, and lacto-vegetarians as a main course.

Char Bar goes far beyond the usual salad, fries, onion rings, and pickles. They have those, plus charred romaine; iceberg wedge; roots & fruits; corn-bread muffins; cheesy "hush puppies"; fried green tomatoes; charred eggplant; creamed asparagus; "pig tail" mac & cheese; cabbage slaw; carrot-raisin slaw; kale-pecorino slaw; smoked corn succotash; beer-battered pickles; jalapeño cheesy corn bake; Anson Mill cheddar grits; broccoli rice casserole; wood-fired portabella grains galore sandwich with charred eggplant, goat cheese, cara-melized onion, roasted red pepper, and arugula; or a smoked jackfruit sand-wich with melted provolone, sliced avocado, and fried jalapeños in an egg bun; and my favorite sourdough grilled pimento cheese sandwich.

Char Bar managing partners, Mark Kelpe and James Westphal, have a proven track record of introducing successful dining concepts to Westport with their popular Beer Kitchen, McCoy's Public House, and The Foundry. Thanks to them, the barbecue void that happened more than a decade ago when John and Rosie Grant turned out the lights at Westport Bar-B-Que is over.

Kelpe and Westphal transformed a big chunk of the former Beaumont Club into a barbecue joint with retro-contemporary ambience. You can't miss the huge mural painted on the cinder block wall in the distance to your left as you walk in. Reminiscent of barbecue graphics in cookbooks, magazines, and postcards from America's 1950s backyard barbecue boom, a proud pitmaster shows off his rotisserie chickens to an admiring female guest. While you and friends sip on libations of craft beers, sodas, infused tea, infused lemonade, or bourbon cocktails, try coming up with the most outrageous or entertaining story to explain what's going on in that scene. If stretching your creative brain cells doesn't appeal to you, other indoor amusements are at hand—foosball and televised sports events. Outdoor amusements such as volleyball and croquet are available for warm weather fun.

While the mural reflects the retro-contemporary Char Bar spirit, the menu goes far beyond 1950s-style backyard fare with a creative medley of Southern-style comfort foods.

The meat menu is crafted by award-winning competition pitmaster Mitch Benjamin, known in Kansas City for his Meat Mitch barbecue sauces. Mitch cooks contemporary competition-style barbecue unlike 1950s backyard barbecue.

My favorite meats in the Whomp Platter are the burnt ends, brisket, and ribs—although the latter leans toward the barbecue competition sweet standard. The ribs are tender and juicy with a hint of hican smoke when you get past the sweetness. The sliced turkey breast is best with a touch of Whomp sauce.

Char Bar's Burnt Heaven sandwich combines ingredients and flavors that befit the name—smoked burnt ends, smoked sausage, fried jalapeños, chipotle barbecue mayo, and creamy slaw. If the egg bun makes the sandwich too large for you to take a bite, dig in with your hands or fork. It is indeed a heavenly combination.

I am also a big fan of the CBGB Burger, made of house-ground smoked brisket, smoked Gouda schmeer, smoked bacon, caramelized onion, and the old Southern favorite Duke's mayo, all on an egg bun.

Their Anson Mills Cheddar Grits rival the famous Garlic Cheese Grits at Miss Mary Bobo's Boarding House in Lynchburg, Tennessee. Touches of cheese and fresh herbal garnish add a tasty color accent.

The Roots & Fruits Salad—roasted beets, parsnips, onion, goat cheese, oranges, pistachios, and crispy brussels sprouts—is a hit with vegetarians and carnivores. Don't let the skull and crossbones warning that "these items contain no meat!!" stop you from enjoying every bite. The combination of ingredients, laced with blackberry wine vinaigrette, resonates deeply within your primal gatherer genes.

The fried green tomatoes, cheesy grits hush puppies, smoked corn succotash, and sweet corn spoonbread are not to be missed. If you have to choose only a few on your first visit, get the fried green tomatoes with tomato chow-chow and mustard sauce, or the cheesy grits hush puppy fritters with beer blanc and jalapeño jam.

Potatoes star in Char Bar's potato salad, hand-cut fries, sweet potato fries, and crispy Jo-Jo's that rival my favorites at Ted's 19th Hole in Minneapolis.

If you have room for dessert, four made-from-scratch options are available: burnt pudding, bourbon peach cobbler, sweet potato funnel cake, and Velvet Elvis.

Kansas City's mix of millennials, Gen Xers, and retirees is a diverse combo of individuals with global culinary interests. All are at home in Char Bar. Although there will always be a demand for the traditional Kansas City barbecue meats and sides that made Kansas City the Barbecue Capital of the World, Char Bar is in step with Kansas City's future.

Cleaver & Cork

1333 Walnut St., Kansas City, MO 64106; (816) 541-3484; www.cleaver andcork.com **Founded:** 2015 **Chef:** Zeb Humphrey **Wood:** Apple for savory foods; cherry for cold-smoked desserts, e.g. crème brûlée

If anyone asks, "Does Kansas City have any high-end, upscale barbecue joints for when you want to really impress a date, spouse, or significant other?", the reply from most Kansas Citians will be, "Try Cleaver & Cork, but plan ahead and make a reservation." It is open for dinner only, from 4 p.m.

"Barbecue joint" isn't a fitting description of Cleaver & Cork. Given its connection with Local Pig's Alex Pope as adviser, and executive chef Andrew Heimburger, collaborator with Pope and formerly at Local Pig, the place has impeccable swine dining credentials. It is high end, fancy by barbecue restaurant standards, and earns consistent high marks from satisfied customers who pack the place nightly.

If your goal is to graze on the few barbecue selections on the menu without making an evening of it, go early. A few featured Happy Hour selections are half price. Barbecue options include smoked pork ribs, slow-smoked pulled pork sandwich, barbecue pork shoulder entree with cornbread, bourbon barbeque sauce, braised red cabbage, or smoked ribeye with Parmesan potatoes and asparagus.

Smoke is also an ingredient in some of the cocktails, the beet sandwich, and the smoked crème brûlée with brandied cherries dessert.

Danny Edwards BLVD BBQ

2900 Southwest Blvd., Kansas City, MO 64108; (816) 283-0880; http://dannyedwardsblvdbbq.com **Founded:** 1980; moved to current location in 2007) **Pitmaster:** Danny Edwards **Wood:** Hickory

Danny Edwards, aka "Lil' Jake," has one of the most iconic pedigrees in Kansas City barbecue. Jake Edwards owned and operated one of the top go-to barbe-

Barbecue Lover's Music, Kansas City Style

Since jazz, blues, and barbecue are part of Kansas City's heritage and image, you'd think that the meat and music genre would be a standard combo throughout the metro area. Not so. Live music in Kansas City barbecue joints is rare these days. Barbecue restaurant soundtracks here feature a variety of jazz, blues, bluegrass, country, red dirt, and pop. Don't count on hearing Bach, Mozart, or Beethoven.

With a few rare exceptions, there's a music scene and a barbecue scene. Seldom do the two scenes converge. When they do, there's a special magic in the air that feeds your soul and bonds you with humankind—past, present, and future. Your body moves to the beat. Your spirit is revived, and even when the music is the blues, you take comfort in knowing that although the blues is your old friend, you're not alone in being on a first-name basis with the nemesis. The music makes it okay to embrace the blues and let it happen instead of fighting it or lamenting it or getting lost in self-pity.

Back when Jim Crow segregation was the norm in Kansas City, the best venues for barbecue and music, especially jazz, were the so-called "twenty blocks of black" on the east side. That's the only place black musicians were welcome to lodge. As a result, when they finished their gigs in the white nightclubs they'd settle into east side clubs for all-night jam sessions. That's where the story about Count Basie's spit ribs emerged. As the story goes, Count Basie was more than irritated when he'd get a slab of barbecue ribs to enjoy during a break, only to find that some or all had disappeared while Count was making music. When he decided to spit on his slab, in public, where all could see, the problem went away.

A more recent music and barbecue venue was the former Grand Emporium on Main Street near 39th Street in Kansas City, Missouri.

Here are your best bets on enjoying live music with your barbecue in Kansas City today:

B.B.'s Lawnside Bar-B-Q
1205 East 85th Street
Kansas City MO 64131
816-822-7427
http://bbslawnsidebbq.com

Knuckleheads Saloon
2715 Rochester St.
Kansas City, MO 64120
(816) 483-1456
www.knuckleheadshonkytonk.com

RJ's Bob-E-Que Shack
5835 Lamar Ave.
Mission, KS 66202
(913) 262-7300
www.rjsbbq.com

Winslow's BBQ
20 E Fifth St.
Kansas City, MO 64106
(816) 471-4727
www.winslowsbbq.com

cue joints in town for many years. During those memorable years he taught son Danny the art, science, and business of barbecue.

Instead of buying his dad's business, young Danny applied the skills learned from his dad, enhanced by his own trial and error, and ventured into business on his own with his extremely popular "Lil' Jake's Eat It & Beat It," downtown. It was a tiny joint, open for lunch only, with seating on 18 stools along 4 rows of narrow Formica counters. Thus, when you got your order you took the first available seat, ate your lunch, and beat it to free up a seat for another customer.

Groans of lament were heard across the continent when Eat It & Beat It was closed to make room for construction of the Power & Light District.

To the applause of his many fans, Danny came back with a new, larger restaurant on Southwest Boulevard, Danny Edwards BLVD BBQ. It has more space and more seating—with tables and chairs—for diners to eat it and beat it at a more leisurely pace. Yet, the new place is so popular that seating is still at a premium at the height of lunch hour, so don't be shy about inviting a stranger holding their lunch with a "Where am I going to sit?" expression to sit on the empty chair at your table. Lifelong friendships can start that way.

Danny serves all of the standard Kansas City barbecue favorites. When I don't get beef and fries or ribs, I go for the burnt ends and sweet potato fries. Danny's Mexican Chili on the winter menu is also a favorite.

"People ask me if I compete. I tell them I compete every day!" Kansas City is glad Danny does compete every day. He is one of our Kansas City barbecue treasures.

Deke's Bar-B-Que

5200 Raytown Rd., Kansas City, MO 64133; (816) 737-9588; http://dekesbar-b-que.com **Founded:** 1989 **Pitmaster:** Dave Williams **Wood:** Peach, hickory, apple, pear, and cherry as available
When you spy Deke's on the side of the road—a small, white with red trim, cinderblock building, custom-printed and hand-painted signs, with a 55-gallon drum smoker pumping out smoke through a crumpled aluminum dryer vent

chimney—you could exclaim, "This is it!" Deke's is the kind of roadside shack many barbecue adventurers have dreamed of finding. Nothing glitzy or fancy, just good, no-frills barbecue and friendly ambience.

And you'll soon learn that Deke's is Kansas City style with a Louisiana accent. David Williams, also known as "Deke," brought his mostly self-taught pitmaster skills from his native Louisiana to Kansas City. He has adapted his style to satisfy Kansas City palates—adding burnt ends and rib tips to his smoked meat repertoire, for example. Yet, fortunately for his many fans, Mr. Williams has not forsaken his Louisiana roots. His authentic signature Louisiana Gumbo—a heavenly medley of chicken, shrimp, crab, rice, corn, okra, tomato, celery, and secret seasonings—draws customers from miles around. Some are none too happy when they arrive with gumbo on their mind and the gumbo is sold out.

A trip to Deke's Bar-B-Que when the gumbo is sold out is not a trip in vain, however. After all, Deke's is first and foremost a barbecue joint. Besides burnt ends and rib tips, Deke's full menu includes chicken, beef, ham, turkey, pulled pork, sausage, big hot links, lamb, hand-cut fresh fries, coleslaw, baked beans, and potato salad. It's so good that you'll still be glad you stopped. Come again another day for the gumbo. If you're still craving a taste of Louisiana, see if Deke's has some red beans and rice on hand. You can fire it up to your preferred level of fieriness with the big bottle of Louisiana Hot Sauce on the counter.

Williams runs Deke's, described by some customers as a "hole-in-the-wall," with occasional help from his wife and son. He is the head pitmaster, using a heavy-duty, custom-built pit from Oklahoma. Depending on what he's cooking and what woods are available, his woods of choice are peach, hickory, apple, pear, and cherry. He has been at it for more than 25 years, so "Deke" knows his way around the pit. He developed his own rub and sauce. He also developed his own sausage recipe and makes the sausage himself. It isn't andouille sausage, but the herbal profile says Louisiana to me. It's good!

Deke's gets especially busy with carryout orders for tailgaters when there's a KC Royals or Chiefs home game. Out-of-towners from opposing teams stop by too, as well as Chiefs and Royals players and fans who have discovered Deke's.

Dave met Kansas City baseball legend Buck O'Neil, but never got an opportunity to serve Buck a plate of Deke's barbecue. Dave's wife, Debra, helps keep the books. Their son, Jason, helps cook and serve when he isn't in school or studying for exams. The Williams family is proudly related to Bob Motley, Congressional Medal of Honor and Purple Heart World War II veteran. Bob is the only umpire from the Negro Leagues era of baseball who is still alive.

There is only one place on Planet Earth where you can count on meeting Dave Williams and eating his barbecue. Dig into a plate and experience Deke's slogan, "Tastes Like More." More what, I asked? Dave said it's an expression from his late father-in-law, a former Negro League player who played on the Gray Ghosts team out of Sioux City, Iowa. More of what you want!

Deke's has been a popular roadside stop for Kansas Citians in the know for almost 30 years. Be sure to call ahead to make sure Deke's is open when you want to stop by. Dave closes the restaurant when he is busy preparing for big catering jobs.

Dickey's Barbecue Pit

9000 NW Skyview Ave., Kansas City, MO 64154; (816) 505-3900; www.dickeys.com **Founded:** 2010 **Pitmaster:** Laura Hammel **Wood:** Hickory

I resolved to avoid including chains in this book. And since the focus is Kansas City–style barbecue, I saw no reason at all to include a chain out of Texas. Here I am, eating my resolve.

After a good friend with Texas roots ate at the Overland Park Dickey's and raved about how good it is, and after another friend told me he was hearing positive remarks about the Skyview Avenue Dickey's, I decided to try the one on Skyview Avenue. My friend, Gary Bronkema, stopped to graze while in the area checking out some other barbecue joints. I figured that if it wasn't any good, he might as well share the misery, since he had recommended it.

To our surprise, it is darned good barbecue. And since Kansas City–style barbecue owes a great deal of its heritage to Texas, Dickey's style of barbecue is not a stranger to our palates. We were completely pleased with the brisket, ribs, turkey breast, and pulled pork. Like most places in Texas, the meat is served naked. If you want sauce, three tomato base styles—Dickey's Original, Sweet, and Hot n' Spicy—are available in warming crocks with dippers and plastic sauce cups.

The brisket, sliced Texas-style thick, is a tender, juicy, flavorful combination of natural meat flavors and a kiss of hickory smoke. Thick-sliced turkey breast muscle meat, lightly seasoned with a pepper and salt rub; tender pork spareribs, moist, flavorful pulled pork: it's all good. Homestyle sides include barbecue beans, creamy coleslaw, potato salad, baked potato casserole, Caesar salad, mac & cheese, jalapeño beans, green beans with bacon, potato chips, fried okra, fried onion "tanglers," and waffle fries.

Laura Hammel, owner/operator, was trained at Dickey's Barbecue University before opening her Kansas City restaurant. She obviously studied hard and learned her lessons well. She proves it, one plate at a time.

The Filling Station Bar-B-Q Restaurant

333 SE Douglas St., Lee's Summit, MO 64063; (816) 347-0794; www.thefillingstationbbq.com **Founded:** 2009 **Pitmaster:** Jill Davolt **Wood:** Hickory

Don't expect to fill up your car's gas tank here. That amenity is long gone with the days when a free windshield cleaning and oil check came with a fill-up in downtown Lee's Summit.

The Filling Station cashes in on nostalgia with barbecue beef, pork, ribs, turkey, sausage, burnt ends, rib tips, smoked catfish, and sides in a funky 1950s setting. Enjoy a Moon Pie, Cherry Mash, brownie, or cobbler—when in season—for dessert while portraits of James Dean and John Wayne look on.

Fiorella's Jack Stack Barbecue

Martin City, 13441 Holmes Rd., Kansas City, MO 64145-1445; (816) 942-9141; multiple locations listed at the end; www.jackstackbbq .com/about-us/a/15 **Founded:** 1947, as Smoke Stack by Fiorella family (original Jack Stack in Martin City opened in 1974) **Pitmasters:** Tim Keegan & pit crews **Wood:** Hickory

Jack Fiorella remembers his childhood days when his parents and siblings lived upstairs in the original storefront Smoke Stack barbecue restaurant founded by his family in 1957. The abandoned building still stands in south Kansas City on Prospect Avenue, for sale—a remarkable piece of Kansas City barbecue history.

Jack grew up learning the business and art of barbecue from his dad, Russ, and staff. By 1974 Jack and his wife, Delores, opened their own barbecue restaurant in Martin City. The popular flagship Jack Stack is still active with enthusiastic diners to this day, joined by the four other Jack Stack restaurants throughout the Kansas City metro area. Today, under the capable leadership of Jack's son-in-law, Case Dorman, Jack Stack's restaurants, catering services and nationwide shipping operation comprise the barbecue industry's largest full-service wood smoked meats restaurant, catering, and shipping business.

Each Jack Stack restaurant has a different decor and feel, yet the menu and appointments such as a horned brass steer leave no doubt that you are in a Jack Stack establishment. The food is consistently good, including all of the Kansas City favorites plus a signature smoked prime rib appetizer and fantastic lamb ribs. I often get a loaded baked potato topped with pulled pork or burnt ends with a salad. It is delicious and more than filling. Jack Stack grilled steaks are some of the best in the city. Jack Stack is a mandatory stop for barbecue lovers who want the full Kansas City–style experience.

Additional locations:

Country Club Plaza, 4747 Wyandotte St., Kansas City, MO 64112-1612; (816) 531-7427

Freight House, 101 W. 22nd St., Kansas City, MO 64108-1954; (816) 472-7427

Overland Park, 9520 Metcalf Ave., Overland Park, KS 66212-2212; (913) 385-7427

1840 NW Chipman Rd., Lee's Summit, MO 64801-3938; (816) 621-7427

Fritz's Meats & Superior Sausages

10326 State Line Rd., Leawood, KS 66206; (913) 381-4618; www.fritz kcmeats.com **Founded:** 1927 **Pitmasters:** Kurt McDonald, Andy C, Josh M **Wood:** Hickory

"Kansas City's oldest smokehouse, "Fritz's has been a Kansas City favorite since 1927. Besides being a huge purveyor of meats, smoked or not, they are a

Sandwiches Kansas City Style

Barbecue joints all over the country feature a variety of creative sandwiches. I have many favorites in other cities. Here's my list of Kansas City favorites.

Z-Man at Joe's Kansas City: This one has skyrocketed to fame and favor since it was introduced in the waning years of the 20th century. It features sliced barbecue brisket, smoked provolone, barbecue sauce, and a couple of onion rings on a bun. You can choose other meat options, but brisket is the original and it's what you'll get unless you order otherwise.

The Remus at Johnny's Barbecue: Spicy or mild house-made pimento cheese topped with Southern-style barbecue pulled pork, sauce, house slaw, a sprinkle of rub, and dill pickle chips on a bun.

Big D at Danny Edwards BLVD: Barbecue beef brisket slices from point, swiss cheese, and two onion rings on marble rye.

Jesse James Melt at Jon Russell's: Smoked turkey, grilled onions, and cheddar cheese.

Jon Russell: Chopped burnt ends and sausage.

KC Smoke Steak Sandwich at Woodyard: "Philly" with smoked brisket, bacon, onion, and Pepper Jack.

Hayward's Pit Master: One pound of lean sliced barbecue beef brisket on a toasted Roma Bakery sesame seed bun, with your choice of one side. For big appetites!

Rickbo at Ricky's Pit Bar-B-Q: A four meat combo.

The Duke at All Slabbed Up: Four slices of toast, layered with your choice of three barbecue meats. Stop talking and eat it, as John Wayne might say.

Ultimate Destroyer at Papa Bob's: Half-pound layers of hickory-smoked pulled pork, sliced pork, sliced ham, turkey breast, three half-pound hamburgers, sliced brisket, sausage, bread, and sauce layers, in a 12-inch hoagie bun, with a half-pound of fries and your choice of four pickle spears, four jalapeño peppers, or two of each. Many have tried, few have eaten it for free in 45 minutes or less.

Non-Meat Sandwiches Kansas City Style

Grilled Pimento Cheese at Char Bar: Served in a barbecue joint that respects vegetarians, this sandwich is good enough to distract a pending vegetarian from going for the meat! Fried green tomatoes, avocado, melted Tillamook cheddar, homemade pimento cheese, in toasted sourdough bread. I love it!

Jackknife at Char Bar: Smoked jackfruit, melted provolone, sliced avocado, fried jalapeños in an egg bun.

Wood-Fired Portabella at Char Bar: Charred portabella, eggplant, goat cheese, caramelized onion, roasted red pepper, and arugula on toasted Grains Galore bread.

Portobello Z: Man at Joe's Kansas City. Available by request.

popular place for lunch. The barbecue is not only delicious, it is some of the lowest priced in town.

Their barbecue features chicken, ribs, brisket, sausage, pulled pork, and ham. I fell in love with the Bette Rogers Sandwich at first bite. It's a heavenly combo of barbecue brisket, ham, and bacon with artichoke mayo, spicy mustard, and roasted red peppers. Bette Rogers of Kansas City entered her masterpiece in Fritz's sandwich competition a few years ago, and won.

Fritz's is an established name in Kansas City barbecue history. Don't miss it.

Gates Bar-B-Q

World Headquarters, 4621 The Paseo, Kansas City, MO 64110; (816) 923-0900; multiple locations listed at the end; www.gatesbbq.com
Founded: 1946 **Pitmaster:** varies by location; all trained at Gates College of Bar-B-Que Knowledge **Wood:** Hickory

Your Kansas City barbecue experience is not complete if you haven't tried Gates. It is all over town. It has endured as a Kansas City barbecue favorite since 1946 and is still going strong.

Besides their barbecue, Gates signature barbecue sauce has wide appeal. It is so popular that it is available in gift stores, grocery stores, and supermarkets throughout the metro area and beyond. It is a masterful blend of tomato concentrate, high-fructose corn syrup, distilled vinegar, salt, onion powder, garlic powder, natural flavors, sugar, celery, spices, and pepper—as listed on the label of the Original Classic sauce bottle— and is more sour than sweet, with an up front taste of tomato and celery, finished with a hint of cayenne and black pepper. Besides the Classic Original, you can get Sweet, Mild, or the award-winning Extra Hot.

First timers should be prepared to hear the trademark, "Hi, may I help you?" as soon as you enter and before you have a minute to study the menu. If you take pride in being prepared, practice saying, "Yes, beef and fries please," or "Yes, short end, beans, and fries please," or whatever else you've decided after reviewing the menu online before you step inside. If you aren't familiar with the menu and you don't know what you want until you study the menu, take your time and order what sounds good to you.

Besides the usual beef, pork, chicken, turkey, ham, sausage, and pork ribs, Gates is one of the few places that offers mutton.

Say "Gates" to a native Kansas Citian and most will reply, "barbecue." Those two words enjoy a long history in this town. The Gates presence, historically and in today's competitive market, is big, powerful, and here to stay. Thousands of Kansas Citians can't last a full week without a taste of Gates barbecue to sustain them. Former Kansas Citians and others who have visited our city and gotten hooked by the Gates signature flavors and mystique have ribs and beef and sauce delivered overnight to their homes or offices on a regular basis. It scares me to think of what would happen to the mental health of a substantial portion of our citizenry if Gates turned out the lights and shut down the pits. Happily, we need not waste emotional energy on such worries.

Gates Bar-B-Q, formerly branded as Gates & Sons, has permanently imprinted an image and a greeting in the minds of Kansas Citians. The image is a graphic of a trim gentleman, dressed to the nines in a vintage striped tuxedo, black and white tuxedo shoes, bow tie, and stovepipe hat, cane cradled in

his right arm, carryout box of Gates barbecue in the other, "Struttin' with some barbecue," presumably in step with the Louis Armstrong jazz instrumental of that title.

My favorite at Gates is the beef sandwich with fresh cut fries. Other Gates regulars swear by the ribs. Still others go for the chicken, turkey, sausage, or mutton. Locals can eat their way through the entire menu, trying something new on each visit, to decide what they like best. Visitors should start with beef and/or ribs the first time.

Gates is all over town. You won't be believed if you live here and haven't tried Gates. Visitors will also be expected to have tried Gates. Everyone has an opinion about Gates barbecue, so you'd best strut with some, eat it, and be prepared to share your own opinion.

Additional locations:

1221 Brooklyn, Kansas City, MO 64127; (816) 483-3880

1325 E Emmanuel Cleaver Blvd., Kansas City, MO 64110; (816) 531-7552

10440 E 40 Hwy., Independence, MO; (816) 353-5880

3205 Main, Kansas City, MO 64111; (816) 753-0828

103rd & State Line, Leawood, KS 66206; (913) 383-1752

1026 State Ave., Kansas City, KS 66102; (913) 621-1334

Guy & Mae's Tavern

119 W William St., Williamsburg, KS 66095; (785) 746-8830 **Founded:** 1973 **Pitmaster:** Ty Thompson **Wood:** Hickory

Williamsburg is not in metropolitan Kansas City. It isn't even close enough to be called an outer ring suburb of Kansas City. So why feature an unpretentious tavern in a small town, population 392, on the Kansas prairie at least an hour's drive from Kansas City, in a book about Kansas City barbecue? Because G&M's signature fall-off-the-bone hickory smoked ribs rubbed with Guy's secret

"hookey poo" rub and Mae's sweet tomato base sauce on the side have attracted Kansas City barbecue lovers by the thousands for more than four decades. "Our little town doesn't have enough people to support this place," a regular local customer told me. "On Friday and Saturday nights the place is packed," he said.

If you didn't bring cash, perish the thought of borrowing autographed dollar bills from the walls and ceilings of Guy & Mae's Tavern. If you don't have a credit card to use in the ATM, or a checkbook with proper ID, you could talk with Judy or Ty or Lori about maybe splitting hickory logs or washing dishes in exchange for your lunch or dinner. Best not to count on doing dishes or chopping wood, however. Plan ahead and bring cash or plastic.

Besides Kansas Citians, Guy & Mae's attracts customers from Lawrence, Topeka, and as far away as Manhattan, Kansas. Thanks to the magic of barbecue, school rivalries between Jayhawks, Ichabods, and Wildcats are set aside at Guy & Mae's. The barbecue is so good that

Pitfalls in BBQ Joints

Pitfalls are not unique to KC BBQ joints. They are everywhere. They are not frequent, but they exist. In defense of pitmasters and barbecue restaurant managers, it is no wonder that pitfalls happen. It isn't easy to juggle the many variables required to turn out consistently good quality barbecue.

Keep in mind that you are doing the establishment a favor by calling them on a pitfall. Most customers, instead of calling the pitfall to management's attention, never come back, and tell their friends and associates why they will never go back. That kind of reaction can lead to the demise of a restaurant. If no one speaks up, management thinks customers are satisfied with what they're doing.

When you're asked, "How is everything?" it's your opportunity to reply with polite candor if you have a problem with the food, ambience, or service. Most managers will appreciate and value your candor. Those who don't will not likely see you again in the restaurant.

Below are some pitfalls I think are important to address:

- The meat is cold. I mean cold, like it came straight out of the refrigerator.
- You forgot to order the meat dry, with sauce on the side. It is drowned in so much sauce that you can't taste the meat.
- Fries are limp, not crispy; cold; or way too salty.
- Table service or counter service is inefficient, rude, or otherwise unacceptable.
- Table is dirty.
- Meat is bitter from excessive smoke.
- Meat is tough and chewy.
- Food is too salty.
- Music is so loud it distracts you from food and conversation, unless you're in a music venue where music with your barbecue is the focus.
- Music doesn't fit the scene. If Beethoven, hip hop, pop rock, or Tiny Tim doesn't enhance your barbecue dining experience, tiptoe out the door.
- Restaurant is noisy due to poor acoustics and/or loud diners.

Guy and Mae Kesner were recognized as Kansas brews and ribs royalty when the late Dave Kratzer, editor of the former *KS Magazine*, proclaimed Guy & Mae's Tavern "The Best BarBieCue Joint in Kansas" in the Winter 1985 edition.

Thanks to the Kesner offspring, G&M's famous ribs are still smoking and the beer is as cold as ever. Before their passing, Guy made sure his rub recipe stayed in the family, and Mae taught son-in-law Ty Thompson her pitmaster techniques.

Mae also kept her secret sauce recipe in the family. To me, Mae's unique original sauce resembles an accidental cousin to Newman's Own Marinara Sauce married to Minnesota's Rudolph's Original Bar-B-Que Sauce. Guy's hookey poo enhances the signature flavor in G&M's smooth, uncomplicated, tomato base sauce that perfectly complements the hickory smoked ribs.

Like Mae's sauce, the menu is uncomplicated. You're here for barbecue and beer. Ribs are mandatory unless you're a vegetarian along for the ride. If so, your options include hot pickles, coleslaw, potato salad, and potato chips. Besides pork ribs, you can get ham, beef, turkey, or Polish sausage. I always get the ribs and BBQ beans. When I add a sandwich, I really like the Polish sausage or a half sausage/half beef combo.

Before your slab or half slab is served, keep in mind that Guy and Mae opened the tavern in 1973, long before the barbecue contest scene in Kansas City heated up. Neither one had a barbecue contest or barbecue restaurant pedigree. Guy was an industrial welder by trade, traveling around the country for various welding jobs, prior to managing the FINA station Red Rooster Truck Stop, where Mae worked as a waitress. Mae's customer service savvy was also sharpened by a former job in a five & dime store. It didn't take them long to get up to speed on smoking ribs and running a barbecue joint in a tavern.

G&M ribs are served naked, seasoned with hickory smoke and hookey poo, topped with a few slices of white sandwich bread, on a sheet of aluminum foil and newspapers. A jar of Mae's sauce is available on the side. Don't expect neatly trimmed ribs like you'd find in a contest entry box. Although Guy & Mae's fall-off-the-bone slabs are sliced by Ty with a sharp knife, they are for eating, not contest-style presentation.

Sit at the long bar, at the picnic table, or in a booth. For 50 cents, the e-jukebox will play a song of your choice. How about eating Guy & Mae's ribs while George Jones sings "There's Nothing Better Once You've Had the Best." Dig in with gusto!

Hank Charcuterie

1900 Massachusetts St., Lawrence, KS 66046; (785) 832-8688; http://hankmeats.com **Founded:** 2014 **Pitmaster:** Vaughn Good **Wood:** Blend of hickory and apple

Vaughn Good learned the art and science of charcuterie, which includes how to smoke meat, at the prestigious International Culinary Center in New York. His place is aptly named a charcuterie, like Kansas City's Local Pig. Since Vaughn, like Local Pig's Devin Campbell, includes smoked meats that resonate with Kansas City barbecue lovers' palates in his repertoire, I think of Hank and Local Pig as barbecue joints with a fused Midwestern French pedigree.

Chef Good offers occasional sessions on how to properly butcher a whole hog, goat, or lamb. He also teaches the basics of sausage making.

Not to worry if you're not interested in charcuterie classes. You can enjoy the bounty from Chef Good's expertise right there in the shop or at home. He offers a full selection of top-quality, locally sourced meats, plus a variety of house-prepared dishes ready to eat.

My advice: Do both. Eat a prepared meal at Hank and buy some meats, sausages, pickles, and seasonings to enjoy at home. Hank's garlic pale ale sausage, chorizo, and andouille take well to grilling. Hank's Tellicherry Rye Peppercorns add fantastic flavor on scrambled eggs, Jo-Jos, and all other foods that you ordinarily pepper. The peppercorns are infused with rye whiskey and smoked over pecan wood. I love the flavor!

Vaughn's mission is to help put Lawrence, Kansas, his hometown, on America's culinary map. He is new to the Kansas City metro barbecue/culinary scene, but is off to a great start!

When you hunger for top-quality, locally sourced meat, or a butchery lesson from an expert, or a slice of delicious pork rib meat pie with roasted brussels sprouts, or duck breast ham, or other smoked charcuterie delights, go to Lawrence. It is worth the trip!

By the way: if you're wondering, as I did, "Where's Hank?" Vaughn will politely explain, "Hank is the charcuterie term for a hundred yards of sausage casing." You already knew that, right?

Hawg Jaw Que & Brew

4403 NW Gateway Ave., Riverside, MO 64150; (816) 741-4294; www.hjfbbq.com **Founded:** 2000 **Pitmaster:** Catherine Thompson **Wood:** Cherry

It's a good sign when workers in bright fluorescent orange or green vests are standing outside having a post-lunch discussion and smoke break before

going back to work. Who and what you see in a parking lot outside a barbecue joint are a good indicator of the quality of the barbecue inside. At Hawg Jaw Fritz BBQ on any given day you could see pickup trucks, late model sedans and SUVs, and a few 1960s or '70s clunkers with sagging bumpers, dented fenders, and shattered brake light covers fixed with red duct tape.

Inside, the mix of businesspeople in suits, retirees in leisure clothes, and road crews in work attire is a good indication that you'll like the barbecue.

Brothers Nick and Sam Silvio, with their sister, Gina, bought the restaurant from the original owners, Bud and Marley Laub. Bud and Marley retain 10 percent ownership. Contest trophies and ribbons, along with pig art, posters, framed photos, oversized tableware, and 1950s road trip memorabilia add eye candy to the indoor restaurant ambience.

The Silvio family kept the name because they like it, and because it's the nickname of a real person, now deceased. Bud and Marley originally planned to name the restaurant after their competition barbecue team name, Porky's Last Stand, until they discovered that a restaurant in Naples, Florida, already has the name. After much discussion, they settled on the nickname of a local Missouri bootheel legend where they both grew up, "Hawg Jaw Fritz." Bud and Marley thought her name would bring them luck. The Silvio siblings thought likewise and kept the name. Marley told me that lots of truckers and others from southeastern Missouri, who spy the name, pull over for pictures. Some stay for the barbecue.

The Silvio family retained pitmaster Catherine Thompson, one of the original Hawg Jaw Fritz pitmasters. Nick is pitmaster when Catherine is not around. He knows fire and smoke. In his other life he's a firefighter. The Silvio family also owns and operates Em Chamas, a successful Brazilian BBQ restaurant in Kansas City's northland.

Hawg Jaw Fritz uses a Southern Pride smoker. They smoke with cherry wood. Bud and Marley Laub's original mild and spicy barbecue sauces are featured, along with one of Nick's own sauces he calls Boss Man's Sauce.

The customers and parking lot at Hawg Jaw Fritz fit a desirable profile. The barbecue stands up to the excellence bar, with variables as at most places—meaning some items are better than others, given differences in individual taste. My favorites are the beef, ribs, burnt ends, sausage, and pulled pork. The beef is tender, with a kiss of smoke. The pork spareribs are top notch, with bark, tender meat, and a kiss of smoke. The burnt ends are tender cubes of brisket with a hint of smoke, no bark. The thinly sliced sausage is mildly spicy, flavorful, with a hint of smoke. I like a touch of Boss Man's Sauce with the pulled pork. The pit beans and seasoned crispy fries are my favorite sides: fantastic!

Besides water, iced tea, and soda, 30 different brands of bottled microbrews, plus 15 small batch root beers are on the beverage menu.

How Hawg Jaw Fritz's nickname came about is an untold tale, but today in Kansas City the name stands for darned good barbecue!

Hayward's Pit Bar B Que

11051 S Antioch Rd., Overland Park, KS 66210; (913) 451-8080; http://haywards-bbq.com **Founded:** 1973 **Pitmaster:** Eric Sweeney and Roland Stephens **Wood:** Hickory & oak

After a successful run at his original location at 95th and Antioch, Hayward Spears moved to the current location at College Boulevard and Antioch to make room for more customers and be more accessible to the booming business and residential population along the College Boulevard corridor. It was a wise decision. Former loyal customers returned to the new location along with an explosion of new customers.

Hayward is the best pitmaster I know who exemplifies the importance of building customer loyalty by producing quality barbecue and knowing your customers by name. In Mr. Spears's case, that would be more than 3,000 customers he knows by name. A good deal of his success came from attention

to details—thousands of details, from staying on top of the inventory, vendor relations, and public relations, right down to making sure each order is plated exactly to his standards, no exceptions. Hayward's is one of the great success stories in Kansas City barbecue.

When Mr. Spears semi-retired and his children were not interested in taking over the business, it had some ups and downs. That is, until a former 13-year-old who, in the early 1970s, used to feed logs in Hayward's pit, grew up and bought the business from Hayward in 2014.

Eric Sweeney, the new owner, has the background, ideas, and experience to move Hayward's forward to its competitive niche among the Kansas City barbecue greats. Eric and pitmaster Roland Stephens served as production manager and pitmaster, respectively, when Joe's Kansas City was growing in fame and recognition as Oklahoma Joe's.

Sweeney is committed as much as possible to the fresh and local emphasis in the national and Kansas City culinary scene. For example, Hayward's produce for salads and some other sides is purchased at the Overland Park Farmers Market in downtown Overland Park, open spring through late fall. The restaurant has undergone some minor renovations under Sweeney, but the original JR Smoker pits are there to stay, churning out hickory and oak smoked ribs, burnt ends, brisket, chicken, pulled pork, and turkey. My favorite continues to be the burnt ends and babyback ribs with Hayward's pit beans and sweet potato chips.

Sweeney's X-Factor is his rapport with and respect for Mr. Spears, who stops by the restaurant almost daily to say hello to familiar customers and make himself available for mentoring whenever Sweeney has questions or asks for feedback. If you've been a loyal customer over the years, it's guaranteed that Mr. Spears will remember you.

HHB BBQ – Hog, Herd & a Bird

906 S Kansas Ave., Topeka, KS 66612; (785) 249-3359; www.hhbbbq .com **Founded:** 2012; started catering in 2009 **Pitmaster:** Eddie Moege **Wood:** Oak

Until Hog, Herd & a Bird made the scene, downtown Topeka hadn't seen a barbecue rib or smelled meat fire smoke since the late Big Will Wright closed the doors to his popular joint in the late 1990s. It was a long time coming, but Kim and Eddie Moege finally filled the gap. When Eddie fires up his vintage homestyle Traeger on the sidewalk in front of HHB, there is no doubt whatsoever that smoke is blowing in the capital city of Kansas. We're not talking about the smoke that blows in the legislative and executive branch offices beneath the capitol dome. We're talking meat smoke.

Eddie was inspired to go into the barbecue business after competing at a KCBS-sanctioned contest at a K-State game in Manhattan, Kansas. He started out doing catering jobs, and then he and Kim decided to take the leap and open a business in downtown Topeka. After a fire destroyed their original location, they moved down the street to the current, larger space. The menu and rustic decor sprinkled with pig art feels like the old place, only better.

"IF IT'S SMOK'N WE'RE OPEN" reads HHB's big sign out front. HHB's smoke smells so good that if the huge fiery-eyed abolitionist John Brown depicted in John Steuart Curry's iconic mural in the state capitol building could suddenly come to life, he would eschew the capitol smoke and go straight to South Kansas Avenue for sustenance at Hog, Herd & a Bird. There he would be treated to exemplary Kansas hospitality and better smoked meats, sides, and beverages than he ever enjoyed back in the day.

HHB is a family-run business that reflects the values, personalities, creativity, and sense of humor of the Moege family. I think John Brown would chuckle after getting past his initial shock and righteous red-faced reaction to Kim's remark, "We serve our barbecue naked." Naked in barbecue lingo means meat with no sauce on it. That's how many barbecue lovers prefer it: fresh from the pit, no sauce. Try it naked first. If sauce is on the table, put a little sauce on your next bite. If the sauce doesn't complement the meat—you're the judge of that—eat it naked.

The HHB menu features pulled pork, brisket, turkey, babyback ribs, chicken, chicken wings, cheesy taters, mac & cheese, smoked baked beans, steamed green beans, coleslaw, smoked corn, potato salad, pasta salad, potato chips, brisket chili, smoked chicken noodle soup, smoked ham and bean soup, and cheesy potato soup. Daily specials, Monday through Friday, are: smoked cheeseburger and side, smoked brat or pork burger and side, half chicken and side, chicken salad on a croissant and side, and quarter slab babyback ribs and side. Specials may vary from week to week.

Beef brisket is tough breast muscle. It is the toughest meat in the barbecue food group, and is more challenging to smoke until tender than it is to pass a bill in the Kansas legislature with 100 percent yeas. Eddie gets it done. Some of my barbecue buddies would say his brisket is pot roast tender, but I say it's darned good fall-apart tender. It is lean, not mushy. The barbecue in this joint is delicious with or without a splash of HHB original or spicy sauce.

HHB's pulled pork is juicy and tender. Some competition-style aluminum foil wrapping may be going on here because the bark isn't crunchy. It is smoke-kissed delicious anyway, naked or sauced.

Unlike their Kansas City neighbors, HHB goes Memphis style with their ribs: babybacks only, no spares. Memphians would call them wet ribs, not naked or showered with "dry sauce," as my friend the late Charlie Vergos called his dry rub at the Rendezvous.

Go for whatever meets the mood of your palate at HHB. They will not disappoint. Don't pass up the brisket chili when available, and try the cheesy taters on the side. John Brown missed out on HHB. That needn't be your fate.

Hickory Log Bar-B-Q

5047 Welborn Ln., Kansas City, KS 66104; (913) 287-9560; **Founded:** 1987 (current owners; original owner opened in 1976) **Pitmaster:** Adam Novosel **Wood:** Hickory

Mention Hickory Log barbecue to anyone who grew up in Wyandotte County and you are likely to hear nostalgic stories. Many remember dining there as children. Some went there on their first date. Families have gathered there for special occasions, especially after Adam and D. Novosel expanded the dining area. The Novosels kept the same rustic, stained knotty pine ambience that longtime customers remember. It has a cozy, welcoming feel, and the barbecue is pure comfort food.

The barbecue is traditional Kansas City–style ribs, beef, pork, ham, sausage, and burnt ends with sides of coleslaw, beans, fries, and garlic toast, served as plated dinners or sandwiches. The slaw, on the sour side of the coleslaw continuum, is an especially good complement to the pork. I especially like the ribs, burnt ends, beans, and fries. The relaxing atmosphere and friendly service are big pluses.

The last time I was there Mr. Novosel told me that he and his wife are ready to retire and enjoy family fun with grandchildren as soon as they can find a buyer who

will continue the Hickory Log tradition. Here's wishing them the best, with applause for their exemplary stewardship of a Kansas City favorite over the past several decades.

Hillsdale Bank Bar-B-Q

201 Frisco St., Hillsdale, KS 66036; (913) 783-4333; http://hillsdale bankbarbq.com **Founded:** 1989 **Pitmaster:** Greg and Donna Beverlin **Wood:** Hickory

The restaurant is open Thursday through Sunday, spring through fall; check the website for dates and hours.

Kansas City residents and visitors who hunger for an authentic taste of no-frills Heartland America barbecue go to Hillsdale Bank Bar-B-Q to get their fix. Hillsdale, population 229, is less than an hour from metro Kansas City. It is worth the trip. Most routes from Kansas City will lead you to I-35, exiting on 56 Highway, then to Highway 156 past Spring Hill to the Hillsdale/Wagstaff exit. Go right at the exit; turn left at the Hillsdale Bank Bar-B-Que sign. You'll see the restaurant from there.

The original building is a 20-by-30-foot, solidly built structure with 14-inch-thick walls. When co-owners Greg and Donna Beverlin opened for business in 1989, the restaurant could seat 30 at most. Now, thanks to add-on space, including a railroad car caboose dining room, the Beverlins can now seat up to 90 diners.

The building really was a bank before it became a barbecue joint. It made the news in 1926 when two male bank robbers walked in on a spring afternoon. One wielded a 44 revolver, ordered the lone cashier into the vault, and locked him in. After helping themselves to more than $1,000 in cash, gold, and silver, they departed on foot. The cashier used a screwdriver to open the vault door. A manhunt was organized after his call for help, resulting in the capture of the robbers before sunset. All but $231.63 was recovered. Today the former vault houses two restrooms for restaurant guests.

Hillsdale Bank Bar-B-Q dining befits the relaxed and casual dining style that Midwesterners appreciate for lunch or dinner. The food will satisfy any hearty appetite. Ranchers, blue-collar workers, millennials, gen-Xers, and elder boomers from nearby cities and suburbs enjoy dining in the relaxed atmosphere.

My favorite combo is ribs, beef, and pulled pork with coleslaw, fresh-cut fries, and add-on orders of onion rings and beans.

The barbecue bears witness to Greg's pitmaster skills and his love of barbecue. The ribs are lean and tender enough to pull with ease from the bone. The slightly crispy outside and kissed-with-smoke flavor make these ribs among the best authentic traditional Kansas City-style barbecue you'll find anywhere. The pork is as good as any you'll find in Memphis, and the beef rivals the best in Texas. The hot and spicy sausage has a bodacious Texas hot link bite to it that will leave a tingle on your lips, but will do no harm. The smoke-kissed chicken and turkey are juicy, flavorful, and tender.

Hot and mild sauce is provided in squeeze bottles at your table. It is worthy of the meat: sweet, with a touch of Tennessee and Carolina sour. If you don't buy some to take home and later on wish you had, you'll find it in most area supermarkets.

The Bank's plainly labeled barbecue sauce bottles for sale simply say, "The Sauce." It is made in the Bank, one big batch at a time. It is so popular that making it cuts into the leisure hours Greg and Donna expected during winter months when the restaurant is closed. They aren't complaining.

In 2011 they introduced pizza from Greg's hand-built wood-fired pizza oven. It's a big hit with omnivores and vegetarians, made to order as you like it.

Greg also built the brick barbecue pit that adjoins the original bank building. Business has been so brisk that he had to replace the original hand-built pit with the current one. He smokes with 100 percent hickory logs for heat and flavor from an offset brick fire box. The result is tender, naturally flavored barbecue meat that takes well to The Sauce of your choice.

Drink options include Pepsi products, local Lost Trail root beer, tea, coffee, lemonade, milk, orange juice, bottled beer, and wine coolers. If Greg and Donna decide to offer cocktails, I suggest a specialty Screwdriver, the Charles Lee, in honor of the bank cashier who escaped from the vault in the spring of 1926 to foil the robbers.

Hog Wild Pit BBQ

1516 W 23rd St., Suite 200, Lawrence, KS 66046; (785) 842-4100; www.hogwildpitbbq.com **Founded:** 2014 in Lawrence (chain based in Wichita) **Pitmaster:** varies by location **Wood:** Hickory

Hog Wild is setting out to make a name for itself in Kansas. With five locations in Wichita, plus restaurants in Salina, Hutchinson, El Dorado, and Lawrence, they have established a significant footprint in the Sunflower State.

The name and friendly animated pig that appears to be flying without wings make an irresistible invitation to come in and try some barbecue. Lawrence and metro Kansas City customers who respond to the invitation are pleasantly surprised at the quality of this mini-chain's slow-smoked brisket, pulled pork, spicy links, turkey breast, pulled chicken, and ribs. They are tender and juicy as advertised. The menu includes a garden salad with or without meat, loaded giant baked potato with or without meat, potato skins, curly fries, coleslaw, potato salad, baked beans, corn, mashed potatoes and gravy, and mac & cheese.

Joe's Kansas City Original Gas Station Location

3002 W 47th Ave., Kansas City, KS 66103; (913) 722-3366; multiple locations listed at the end; www.joeskc.com **Founded:** 1997 **Pitmasters:** None. They have a "smokehouse crew" at each location **Wood:** Missouri white oak

Joe's Kansas City is the breakthrough exception to the rule that this town is so full of great, longstanding, barbecue empires that a newcomer can't overshadow them all. Jeff and Joy Stehney broke new ground in the Kansas City barbecue

scene when they put their business savvy, capital, and competition barbecue skills in an obscure Shamrock gas station on the Wyandotte County line, catty-corner from Westwood and Roeland Park, Kansas, in Johnson County, and made the whole neighborhood famous in a few short years.

The novelty of barbecue in a gas station was the initial attraction, but the quality of the barbecue is what kept people coming back—so much so that the Joe's empire was expanded to Olathe and Leawood with fancier digs and not a drop of petrol for sale.

The empire began under a different name, "Oklahoma Joe's," forged out of a longtime friendship with Joe Don Davidson, inventor of the famous "Oklahoma Joe" barbecue cookers and a formidable contender in the competition barbecue circuit in his own right. In 2014, in order to differentiate the Kansas City Joe's from the Oklahoma Joe's—two independent barbecue and barbecue sauce enterprises—the Stehneys rebranded the Kansas City business to "Joe's Kansas City." Joe Don Davidson continues his barbecue restaurant, sauce, and seasonings business under the Oklahoma Joe's brand. His flagship restaurant is in Broken Arrow, Oklahoma, with a branch in downtown Tulsa at the legendary Cain's Ballroom. Davidson has plans to expand the Oklahoma Joe's brand to other locations inside and outside Oklahoma.

All of Joe's competition-quality barbecue meats are a big hit with local, national, and international diners. Each dish has its fans. My favorites are the burnt ends, the Carolina Pork Sandwich, and the Z-Man sandwich. The Z-Man, by the way, is also available with smoked portobello mushrooms instead of the traditional brisket. By request you can get it with pulled pork, turkey, ham, or burnt ends on the days burnt ends are available. The seasoned fries, dirty rice, red beans and rice, and smoked chicken gumbo are my favorite sides. I'm not a big fan of the beans, but I'm extra fussy about beans and Joe's beans have their fans.

Joe's has a special facility for private functions in Olathe. Branded as the "180 Room," it is named after the coveted perfect score in Kansas City Barbeque Society–sanctioned contests.

Check Joe's out and see what you think. If the line is outside the doors when you arrive, enjoy visiting with others as your hunger and anticipation builds. It is worth the wait.

Additional locations:

11950 S Strang Line Rd., Olathe, KS 66062; (913) 782-6858

11723 Roe Ave., Leawood, KS 66211; (913) 338-5151

Johnny's Bar-B-Q

5959 Broadmoor St., Shawnee Mission, KS 66202; (913) 432-0777; second location at 1375 W Hwy. 56, Olathe, KS 66061; (913) 768-0777; www.johnnysbbqkc.com **Founded:** 1983 **Pitmasters:** Johnny White, Brian White, Mike Brouhard & Eric White **Wood:** Hickory

Since Johnny White opened his Mission flagship barbecue restaurant in 1983, it has become one of the most popular barbecue joints in Kansas City.

Johnny is one of several local pitmasters who learned the art and business of barbecue from Kansas City barbecue legend, the late Anthony Rieke. Johnny cut his barbecue teeth on hand-built, all-brick barbecue pits fired with 100 percent hickory wood.

At age 14 he started learning the trade at Rosedale, all the way from bussing tables to putting orders on the serving counter to feeding the pit and tending the meat. He remembers when the original Rosedale sauce was gritting like the original Arthur Bryant's sauce. Besides Mr. Rieke, Johnny attributes his early learning of the barbecue method of cooking to the late Fatty Sharp. Fatty regaled young Johnny with many stories in addition to imparting his barbecue wisdom.

By 1978 Johnny went full-fledged into the barbecue business on his own, opening the very successful Santa Fe Barbecue in Olathe. After selling it to the Dace family in 1983 he opened Johnny's Bar-B-Q in Mission, Kansas, in a former Straw Hat pizza joint. With the help of his talented wife, Linda, he did a complete makeover from pizza decor to barbecue joint decor, with a mix of Western, Native American, and barbecue contest memorabilia; a huge collection of barbecue sauces from everywhere; and vanity BBQ license plates. Look around and you'll also guess that Johnny likes to fish. You guessed right.

Johnny's menu includes the basic meats you expect in Kansas City: pork spareribs, pork shoulder, beef brisket, chicken, rib tips, and burnt ends. Although the Rosedale influence is noticeable, Johnny has developed his own original style.

Beyond the basics, Johnny offers his signature chili, smoked meatballs with pasta or in a sandwich, or his quarter-pound, all-beef hot dog, splayed, fried, and topped with chili on a hamburger bun. Johnny's signature sandwich, The Remus, with pimento cheese, pulled pork, coleslaw, sauce, rub, and dill pickle chips has become a local favorite. It is named after my barbecue persona, but I'd like it regardless of what Johnny named it.

His beans are some of the best in town. I'm also a big fan of Johnny's coleslaw, a good balance of creamy and sour.

Johnny's beer menu includes the standard major national brands on tap, plus Kansas City's Boulevard Wheat. As demand for craft beers escalates, Johnny will add more brands.

His award-winning all-purpose rub will up your barbecue game.

Johnny's team includes his son Eric, who runs Johnny's in Olathe; Brian White, Johnny's brother; Mike "Bubba" Brouhard, Johnny's brother-in-law; Terri Brouhard, Johnny's sister; Shannon Hammer, Johnny's niece; plus longtime dining room staffers Jason Ossana and Jan Monty.

Jon Russell's Kansas City Barbeque

12094 W 135th Street, Overland Park, KS 66221; (913) 213-6944; www.jonrussellsbbq.com **Founded:** 1997 (in current building since 2007) **Pitmaster:** Luther Saulsbery **Wood:** Hickory

Jon Russell's – West (takeout only – limited menu)

(Located inside Prairie Market Convenience Store)
9350 Renner Rd., Lenexa, KS 66219; 913-213-5008

What better name for a barbecue joint than a first name combo of two competition barbecue team members who have been best friends for life. Not all combos would work, but many would: Billy Bob's or David Harry's, for example. But Zachary Doug's or Henry Emma's? Perhaps not. Jon Russell's works like a charm as a good name symbolic of an enduring friendship.

Jon Niederbremer and Russell Muehlberger grew up in south Kansas City together, went to the same schools, formed an award-winning competition barbecue team, and eventually developed the Jon Russell's restaurant brand in partnership with 39th Street Bevco of Kansas City LLC, owner. Russell, a Certified Executive Chef, brought extensive restaurant experience to the team. Jon added his management and public relations experience to the launch.

Jon Russell's barbecue is smoked in Ole Hickory pits, using apple wood for long smokes and white oak for short smokes. The menu features standard Kansas City favorites, plus smoked salmon and a signature slab of ribs named in honor of the late legendary Kansas City pitmaster, Karen Putnam, known in barbecue circles as "Flower of the Flames." The ribs are sauced with a raspberry jalapeño sauce inspired by Karen's original recipe. Excellent sides include mac & cheese, white bean chili, pit beans, home fried potato chips, crispy onion rings, and seasoned fries. Jon and Russell have moved on to other enterprises. They can take pride in knowing that their legacy brand is a Kansas City favorite.

Home base is at 135th Street and Quivera, plus satellite locations.

K&M Bar-B-Q

603 N Webster St., Spring Hill, KS 66083; (913) 592-5145; www.kandm bbq.com **Founded:** 1991 **Pitmaster:** Ken Kinler **Wood:** Hickory
Ken and Michelle Kinler are the "K&M" owners of this popular restaurant on the southern outskirts of the Kansas City metro area. They transitioned from selling barbecue at county fairs, festivals, and other events to opening a free-standing restaurant where customers come to them instead of the reverse. They were so successful in their first building that after remodeling several times to accommodate more customers, they moved into the current much larger barn-size structure, appointed with cement floors and lots of wood

inside and out. The logo and indoor decor give K&M a rancher/cowboy ambience. They needed the extra space for parking and seating. It's a busy place.

K&M's hickory smoked barbecue meats—beef, burnt ends, pork, ribs, turkey, ham, and sausage—get high marks on flavor and tenderness. The pork spareribs are traditional untrimmed Kansas City style. I especially like the ribs, burnt ends, and barbecue bowl with pulled pork, sauce, potato casserole, beans, grated cheddar cheese, and a pickle spear.

Catfish lovers flock to K&M on Tuesday nights for fried catfish with hush puppies, slaw, fries, and tomato relish. Fried shrimp is always available as well as smoked salmon. Customers with a big appetite go for the Killer Combo sandwich piled high with a choice of three meats: beef, ham, turkey, pork, or sausage.

K&M's three styles of barbecue sauce—the original tomato base sauce, the sweet heat sauce, and the northern Alabama-style white sauce—are favorites of barbecue lovers all over Kansas City, where it is stocked by many grocers and supermarkets.

THE BBQ JOINTS

LC's Bar-B-Q

5800 Blue Pkwy., Kansas City, MO
64129; (816) 923-4484; **Founded:**
1992 **Pitmaster:** LC Richardson &
pit crew **Wood:** Hickory

When you get within whiffing distance
of LC's barbecue pit you'll know you're in
for some first-rate barbecue.

I first met LC years ago when his reputation was building as the hottest new
barbecue joint in Kansas City. I asked
him what "LC" stands for. "Just LC," he
told me. Later I learned his last name,
Richardson.

LC's big, original, custom-made,
solid steel, brand-new cooling tank
cooker converted for barbecue cooking
used to sit outside in full view sending
its enticing aroma to passing motorists.
He has since retired the original cooker
for an indoor pit.

LC cooks with 100 percent hickory.
"The difference in the barbecue is cookin'
with real wood," he told me. "You cook with real wood, then you have smoke."
Unlike most other Kansas City barbecue pitmasters, LC uses a blast and simmer method of cooking. Instead of smoking his briskets low and slow for 16 to
18 hours, he said, "I've found out with barbecue, you blast it. Then you put it
back and let it rest, let it simmer." LC's blast-and-simmer method yields tender,
juicy, smoke-ringed brisket with bark in 6 to 8 hours. His ribs, chicken, and
sausage take less time. "Cookin' ribs, you got to get them in and out as quick
as possible to keep the juice and moisture," he explained. "Real fast to start,
but not burnt, then let it simmer." He uses a spicy rub and finishing sauce
reminiscent of his Mississippi roots, but toned down with sweetness to appeal
to Kansas City palates. You get a choice of mild or hot.

True to classic grease house standards, LC's interior is nothing fancy—
white paint over cinder block walls. The order counter stands behind you
and the small kitchen. Big clock on the wall. Menu board. Kitchen tables and
chairs. Seats around 30. Order/pay/pick-up. Small. Friendly. No frills.

LC's thrives on rib and beef sales. His blast-and-simmer method yields tender, flavorful morsels of grease house gold. When you're looking for something different, try his Italian sausage with a side order of made-from-scratch fries.

LC told me he fixes his barbecue "the way I would like to eat it." Thousands of other Kansas Citians, including this one, like it LC's way, too.

Local Pig

2618 Guinotte Ave. (East Bottoms), Kansas City, MO 64120; (816) 200-1639; www.thelocalpig.com **Founded:** 2012; Pigwich Food Truck, 2013 **Chef/Butcher:** Alex Pope **Wood:** Apple

Brainchild of butcher and charcuterie expert Alex Pope, Local Pig has established a big footprint on the Kansas City culinary scene. There are two locations—the original in the industrial East Bottoms neighborhood that attracts thousands of live music fans to the nearby Knuckleheads, plus the newer Westport store with sit-down indoor dining and table service. Both locations

Hot Dogs in KC BBQ Joints

The hot dog is not the signature meat in Kansas City barbecue joints. Many places relegate hot dogs to the kids' menu. Nobody makes their own hot dogs in-house. They buy premade, precooked wieners of varying composition. They can be boiled, broiled, grilled, microwaved, or roasted.

Why on earth, then, would the late Julia Child, international culinary icon, love hot dogs? Until I learned otherwise, I thought "Julia Child likes hot dogs" was an oxymoron. After all, she co-authored the classic two-volume *Mastering the Art of French Cooking,* plus other enduring tomes. She pioneered food shows on television. She took food seriously, and was far more than "just a cook." She was a breakthrough graduate of Le Cordon Bleu in Paris, when the prevailing attitude was that women belong in the home kitchen and men belong in the restaurant kitchen.

She loved a cornucopia of culinary delights, and the truth is that she included a love for hot dogs in the mix. She called them "hot dogs," with emphasis on "dogs."

Julia never stepped foot in Kansas City, but if she could miraculously appear here today, I like to speculate about where she would find her favorite while doing a Kansas City barbecue crawl. I know for a fact that she also loved barbecue.

Here are a few hot dogs I wish she could have tried:

Big Dog at Earl Quick's, 1007 Merriam Ln., Kansas City, KS 66103; (913) 236-7228: Half-pound, deep-fried, spiral-cut hot dog loaded with ground beef chili, shredded cheese, and chopped onion. To the regret of thousands of local and out-of-town fans, the restaurant is closed. However, the Big Dog is available at times on the Earl Quick's food truck.

Chili Dog at Johnny's Bar-B-Q, 5959 Broadmoor St., Shawnee Mission, KS 66202; (913) 432-0777; second location at 1375 W Hwy. 56, Olathe, KS 66061; (913) 768-0777; www.johnnysbbqkc.com: One large all-beef, split, deep-fried dog, centered on a hamburger bun, topped with Johnny's ground beef and beans chili, dill chips, sliced purple onion, and pickled jalapeño slices on the side.

Finnie at Woodyard, 3001 Merriam Ln., Kansas City, KS 66106; (913) 362-8000; http://woodyardbbq.com/finnie: Quarter-pound, all-beef smoked hot dog covered with chili and cheese.

Harry S at A Little BBQ Joint, 1101 US-24, Independence, MO 64050; (816) 252-2275; www.alittlebarbqjoint.com: Grilled hot dog topped with pulled pork and Pepper Jack cheese

These hot dogs aside, we know with certainty that if Julia craved hot dogs in Kansas City, a mandatory stop would be Costco for a quarter-pound all-beef dog with mustard, chopped onions, and sauerkraut. Costco's and Nathan's Famous foot-long, all-beef hot dogs were her known favorites. She also reportedly stocked up on airport hot dogs to eat airborne in first class. She would no doubt have savored a fair share of Kansas City's world famous barbecue had we been so fortunate as to host her.

find favor with a mix of ages, genders, and lifestyles in the Kansas City demographic landscape. Local Pig is a combination butcher shop, charcuterie, and dining destination with a few barbecue items on the menu. Their emphasis is on produce and meat from small local farms.

Barbecue items on the menu include a pulled pork burger with barbecue sauce, goat cheese, and slaw, also called a Pigwich; a crispy half pig's head, smoked and paired with roast corn, pickled red onion, salsa verde, loaf of bread, and sriracha; and smoked pork loin with corn, fried onion, and provolone sandwich. When their brisket sandwich topped with onion straws is featured at the stationary Pigwich East Bottoms food truck, don't miss it. Delicious!

Lonnie Q's BBQ

3150 SE 21st St., Topeka, KS; (785) 233-4227; www.facebook.com/lonnieqbbq **Founded:** 2013 **Pitmaster:** Lonnie Weaver **Wood:** Hickory

It is fun to speculate as to why the name of the capital city of Kansas means "a good place to grow potatoes" in the language of the Kansa tribe, the state's namesake. I've put that on my list for further research.

When my friend, Terry Lee, and I found Lonnie and Christine Weaver's Lonnie Q's on semi-wooded prairie farmland next to an RV park on the outskirts of Topeka, the thought crossed my mind that this could be why; it looks like a good place to grow potatoes.

Fortunately for barbecue lovers, Lonnie and Christine are devoted to excellence in barbecue instead of growing potatoes. They do know, however, how to pair potatoes with barbecue. Lonnie Q's cheesy potatoes are fantastic, especially when combined with beans and heaping portions of brisket, pork, and turkey in the overflowing "Cup of Heaven." That cup alone is reason enough to go to Topeka.

As I see it, Lonnie and Christine vie with the Atwood Brothers, Lee and Craig, for designation as the Franklin Barbecue of Topeka. They rarely attract a 2-hour-long wait line like Aaron Franklin in Austin, Texas, but hey, Austin's population is 885,000 plus tourists, and Topeka's is only 127,000, with fewer tourists.

In the tradition of Central Texas pitmasters, Lonnie Weaver is a stick burner. Instead of mesquite or post oak, he burns hickory in his made-in-Oklahoma, heavy-gauge steel pit. When Lonnie told me that he used to be pitmaster at the Harley-Davidson barbecue joint closer to downtown Topeka, I said, "No wonder I like your barbecue! I had many a great lunch at that place and loved it." Brisket, pork, turkey, and ribs comprise the meat menu at Lonnie

Q's, all smoked to perfection. Their registered motto is, "We Smoke It...and It's Legal." Sides include beans, slaw, cheesy potatoes, and chips. It is high-quality, basic, no-frills barbecue fare.

I also learned about another Lonnie talent that was news to me: He's an artist. He painted the music-themed art on the walls at Lonnie Q's, as well as the Lonnie Q's logo.

Lonnie Q's occupies a new brick, glass, and wood freestanding structure with high ceilings and ambience befitting a barbecue joint instead of the RV showroom it formerly housed. It feels friendly inside. The friendliness is contagious, rippling through the restaurant from the serving line and dining tables.

Lonnie Q's opens for lunch at 11, Monday through Friday. The line forms early and is often out the door. Dinner is served on Friday. Lonnie cooks and serves the barbecue. He and his wife don't advertise, but to paraphrase some wisdom from the late William Shawn, longtime editor of the *New Yorker* magazine: Those who are best at what they do needn't engage in self-advertisement. Lonnie Q's exemplifies that wisdom each time the customers line up at the door.

McGonigle's Market

1307 W 79th St., Kansas City, MO 64114; (816) 444-4720; www.mcgon igles.com **Founded:** 1951 (barbecue food truck opened, c. 1992) **Pitmaster:** Mike McGonigle & pit crew **Wood:** Hickory

The barbecue business as we know it today owes a great deal to 19th-century immigrant butchers in Texas and elsewhere who discovered that barbecue turned tough meats customers wouldn't buy for home consumption into tender, flavorful meat that sold for a profit at the market. There was no longer a need to discard it.

The meat market barbecue tradition is still alive and well in Texas, and to a lesser extent in Kansas City, thanks to Fritz's, Bichelmeyer, Werner's, and a few new meat markets.

Owner/president Mike McGonigle at McGonigle's Market on Ward Parkway at 79th Street revived the butcher/pitmaster tradition, a dozen or so years ago when he stoked up his vintage Southern Yankee cooker and some Ole Hickory cookers and went full tilt into the barbecue business.

McGonigle's has been the best-known secret among Kansas City competition barbecue teams for years. Mike hasn't tallied the numbers, but teams in the Great Lenexa BBQ Battle, the American Royal Barbecue, and other metro area contests have purchased tens of thousands of pounds of McGonigle's brisket, pork ribs, pork butt, and chicken over the years. Many credit McGonigle's meat as a key to their success.

McGonigle's is also the place where barbecue sauce makers hope to repeat the KC Masterpiece success story. Legend has it that McGonigle's is one of the prime locations where Dr. Rich Davis market-tested his new KC Masterpiece Barbecue Sauce more than three decades ago. It flew off the shelves and the rest is history. Today KC Masterpiece takes prominent humble space on the bottom row of McGonigle's vast local and national barbecue sauce selections.

To order barbecue at McGonigle's you have to follow Mr. McGoo's 1-2-3 BBQ Rules: (1) order and pay inside; (2) bring receipt to the trailer, and (3) enjoy!

Next Year's Winner BBQ & Catering

Vivion West Shopping Center, 2306 NW Vivion Rd. Northmoor, MO 64150; (816) 587-4227; www.nextyearswinnerbbq.com **Founded:** 2011 **Pitmasters:** Steve Christian **Wood:** Hickory

"We're Smokin' Optimism" sums up the philosophy at Next Year's Winner. Optimism, smoked or unsmoked, is a state of mind I respect. It drives progress. It's contagious. And it's a lot more fun than pessimism.

I wondered why a business with optimism as their philosophy would be named "Next Year's Winner," especially since their competition barbecue team of the same name has been competing at the American Royal World Series of Barbecue ® for more than 20 years. The "next year" notion reminds

How's Mike doing with his own barbecue?

It's good enough to stand alone as a separate business that rivals Kansas City's best barbecue joints. I give Mike's ribs, pulled pork, burnt ends, and brisket sandwiches high marks on appearance, tenderness, and taste. In other words, it looks good, it's easy to chew, and the smoke-kissed meat slathered with Blues Hog sauce make me glad I live in Kansas City.

The cheesy corn, seasoned Parmesan waffle fries, and pit beans are delicious sides.

McGonigle's is rich with Kansas City history. It's a prime example of how the marriage of meat, hardwood, and know-how made Kansas City famous for barbecue. Granted, the meat market/barbecue tradition was already more than four decades old when Bill McGonigle, Mike's father, opened the Ward Parkway market in 1951, continuing Bill's grandfather's meat market legacy going back to 1882. More than five decades after the Ward Parkway market opened, Mike decided to smoke and sell barbecue to go or to enjoy at picnic tables on the grassy, tree-shaded lawn next door. Mike got up to speed quickly.

McGonigle's friendly, efficient, and knowledgeable staff, fantastic selection of top quality meats, and food truck barbecue fresh from the pit make it easy to see why 79th and Ward Parkway is one of the most popular barbecue destinations in Kansas City.

me of a sign at Cooper's Old Time Pit Bar-B-Que in Llano, Texas: "Free Beer. Tomorrow."

Steve Christian, owner/pitmaster, explained the restaurant name this way: Several years ago, he and some barbecue buddies were competing at the American Royal. As has been known to happen, especially on Friday nights at the Royal Barbecue, the team was having such a good time partying that they didn't pay attention to their cooking. Beef brisket, for example, can take up to 18 hours, sometimes more, of low and slow smoking to reach the desired level of tenderness. If you party all night and put your brisket or pork butt in the pit

at sunrise, you risk having tough brisket and butt by turn-in time, even if you wrap the meat in aluminum foil and crank up the heat, in essence steam cooking the meat. When it dawned on them that they were too late to cook a winning entry, someone suggested, "What the heck. Let's be next year's winner." The name stuck, and the team started winning ribbons, trophies, and cash the next year and beyond. One of their most prestigious awards is First Place in Pork at the American Royal in 2010.

When you eat at the restaurant or have your event catered by Next Year's Winner, you'll taste proof that Steve Christian has been tending the pit instead of partying. His ribs, brisket, and pulled pork draw easy maximum Kansas City Barbeque Society (KCBS) 9s on appearance, tenderness, and taste. Customers who routinely stop by for a BBQ Sundae say you can't go wrong with it, a barbecue feast in a jar. The jar is filled with layers of rib tips and barbecue beans, topped with coleslaw and a bacon-wrapped, glazed, smoked meatball as the traditional sundae "cherry." If you don't want to mess with eating it from a jar, order a "deconstructed" sundae.

Besides delicious pit beans and coleslaw, Steve's other popular sides are cheesy potatoes, potato salad, beans, coleslaw, and jalapeño cheesy corn.

Papa Bob's Bar-B-Que

11610 Kaw Dr., Kansas City, KS 66111; (913) 422-4210; http://papabobs bbq.com **Founded:** c. 2007 **Pitmaster:** Bob Caviar **Wood:** Hickory

Bob Caviar, owner/pitmaster at Papa Bob's, is one of the most fun barbecue restaurant proprietors you'll meet in Kansas City. His barbecue—all of the Kansas City standards—is delicious, and I don't know of any other place that features 10 different sauces, each with a distinctly different flavor.

The restaurant looks like a white frame shack outside, with a 1950s and '60s retro feel inside. The most famous sandwich at Papa Bob's is the Ultimate Destroyer for $60, or free if you can clean your plate in 45 minutes or less. Many have tried; few have prevailed. It even got the best of *Man v. Food* TV star Adam Richman.

Bob features fried catfish fillets with hush puppies and slaw every Wednesday. And yes, he's endured a lifetime of kidding about his last name. Maybe learning to laugh at corny puns and teases helps explain his cheerfulness. His grandkids also make him cheerful.

For great food and fun, go see Papa Bob.

Plowboys

3111 S Missouri 7, Blue Springs, MO 64014; (816) 228-7569; second location at 1111 Main St., Suite 115, Kansas City, MO 64198; (816) 221-7569; www.plowboysbbq.com/location.html# **Founded:** 2013 (catering was founded in 2001) **Pitmaster:** Todd Johns & Steve Fennelly **Wood:** White oak

Plowboys is another of the new barbecue joints that transitioned from barbecue contest champions to successful barbecue restaurant owners. In addition to many other awards, Todd and Audrey Johns, with their Plowboys competition barbecue team, are Grand Champions of the 2009 prestigious American Royal World Series of Barbecue Invitational. Three years later Todd and Audrey teamed up with Todd Johnson, chief financial officer, to open the flagship Plowboys Barbeque in Blue Springs.

The pulled pork, brisket, burnt ends, babyback pork ribs, and sausage at Plowboys look great, and are tender, juicy, and most of all, delicious. My personal favorites are the ribs and burnt ends. The kissed-with-smoke ribs are lightly rubbed and sauced, not drowned in overpowering seasonings. The other meats are also lightly seasoned with rub. Sauce is on the side, so you can sauce or not, as you wish.

Plowboys departs from the mainstream Kansas City tradition of serving pork spareribs. Plowboys ribs are meaty babybacks like in Memphis, but with a distinct Kansas City accent. These meaty, lightly seasoned, kissed-with-Kansas-City-smoke ribs rival the best you'll find in Memphis.

Of the sides—two styles of coleslaw, cheesy hashbrowns, regular fries, sweet potato fries, and pit beans—my favorites are the pit beans, both types of fries, and the cheesy hashbrowns. Plowboy's rendition of the Carolina-style sandwich with the pulled pork and coleslaw, fast becoming a fixture in Kansas City barbecue restaurants, is delicious! Their brisket sandwich by itself or with sausage is also a pleaser.

The Kansas City Plowboys is not to be confused with a Plowboys in Marshall, Missouri. Todd Johns's brother-in-law and original competition cooking partner, Randy Hinck, runs that one. Randy uses the Plowboys logo by arrangement with Todd and Audrey.

At Plowboys Blue Springs you order and pay at the counter; pick-up when your number is called. Downtown you'll have your order when you pay at the counter. Service is friendly and efficient in both places.

Don't be surprised if there's a wait line at both locations. Be calm and patient. The line moves right along. Plowboys barbecue is worth the wait.

Q39

1000 W 39th St., Kansas City, MO 64111; (816) 255-3753; www.q39kc.com **Founded:** 2014 **Pitmaster:** Rob Magee **Wood:** Hickory for smoking; oak for grilling

Kansas City barbecue lovers are wowed by the culinary talents of chef/pitmaster/co-owner Rob Magee at Q39.

Besides consistent food quality and signature dishes, Rob knows that a key to success in the barbecue business is customer relations. Whenever possible, Rob leaves the kitchen to table hop and visit with his many fans and

Best BBQ in Kansas City

When word is out that you're writing about Kansas City barbecue, the most frequent question is, "Where's the best?" or "What's your favorite?"

"Best" is 90 percent subjective, even when objective measures such as ambience, quality of service, quality of food, consistency, and other criteria are spelled out.

Comparing ambience in a roadside carryout shack with a fancier table service establishment isn't a fair comparison. It is "objective" only if your measure favors one type of ambience over another.

Or, judging ribs by contest standards—e.g., if the meat falls off the bone, it's overcooked—instead of what customers want at a particular place—e.g., meat that falls off the bones—is another example of where objective and subjective get muddled.

Today's Kansas City barbecue scene is a mix of traditional and new.

I've culled a list that enables you to experience the full spectrum of today's offerings. These places are a good start. Try them and the others in this book. Then let the argument begin among you and your friends as to which is best, while keeping in mind that "best" is mostly subjective and a moving target.

Traditional

Traditional is what made Kansas City famous for barbecue. Each place is different, with signature flavors and standout best dishes. They have stood the test of time. If you haven't tried one, several, or all, you haven't experienced Kansas City barbecue.

Arthur Bryant's (flagship location on Brooklyn Avenue)
Gates
Rosedale
Jack Stack
Snead's
Johnny's
Danny Edward's BLVD

LC's
Wyandot
Zarda's

New

All who are in step with a temporocentric "What's new?" and "What's trending?" focus will not be disappointed at these places:

Slap's
Joe's Kansas City
Plowboys
Q39
Char Bar (vegetarians love this place too!)
Burnt End
The Rub

customers. Many followed him from his previous tenure at Café Wetherby at the Airport Hilton. While there he honed his barbecue skills by competing in and winning at contests with his Munchin' Hogs at the Hilton team.

On your first visit, start with shareable onion straws and mac & cheese with herbed bread crumbs. Buffalo Sweat and Velvet Rooster on tap, brewed by Tallgrass Brewing Co. in Manhattan, Kansas, are a perfect complement.

Rob's barbecue is top notch. I especially like his burnt ends burgers, brisket, pulled pork, and house-made chipotle sausage. The sausage is especially good in Rob's white bean cassoulet, a bowl of beans I always order at Q39. The sausage has a satisfying balance of fat-to-lean that delivers a wallop of flavor without excessive grease. It is meaty and not overspiced. The kiss of smoke and chipotle is a palate pleaser.

A good option to try on your first visit is the Judges Plate of brisket, ribs, pulled pork, and pit beans.

Q39 is upscale urban, not at all snobby, but Rob doesn't call it a joint. Kansas Citians call it a great place for barbecue, and I agree.

Ricky's Pit B-B-Q
3800 Leavenworth Rd., Kansas City, KS 66104; (913) 371-8088;
Founded: c. 1990 **Pitmaster:** Ricky Smith **Wood:** Hickory, apple & oak

Ricky Smith has moved his famous Kansas City barbecue joint a few times over the years. No matter where he moves, his throngs of loyal customers find him. He currently occupies a former ice cream shop on Leavenworth Road, on the fringe of the historic Quindaro neighborhood of pre–Civil War through Reconstruction-era significance.

Ed Asner once called Ricky's barbecue "The Greatest!" President Bill Clinton ate at Ricky's former red-roofed Leavenworth Road location on one of his first Presidential stops in Kansas City. On a wall above the inside entrance, Ricky proudly displays a framed photo of POTUS 42 and himself, shaking hands.

No matter where he's smoking, Ricky's Pit barbecue is consistently good. He offers the standard Kansas City favorites: beef, pork, turkey, ham, sausage, spareribs, burnt ends, and rib tips, with traditional baked beans, coleslaw, potato salad, fries, and onion rings. A popular item for the super-hungry or for sharing a meal is the "Rickbo" sandwich: a four meat combo. Ribs, sausage, and beef are my favorites, with Ricky's slightly spicy beans on the side. He also serves some of the best chili in town, year round.

Not to worry if you forget to order Ricky's barbecue with sauce on the side. He doesn't drown the meat in excessive sauce—a tomato base sauce with a hint of chili seasonings and a cayenne kick that dances well with each meat.

There's no way I could go to Ricky's without eating barbecue, usually until I'm too full for dessert. Not a problem. When there's no room for dessert, take some home to enjoy later. On any given day you could be lucky enough to get a slice of sweet potato pie before it's sold out—or peach cobbler, pound cake, or my all-time favorite, pecan pie.

RJ's Bob-E-Que Shack

5835 Lamar Ave., Mission, KS 66202; (913) 262-7300; www.rjsbbq.com
Founded: 2003 **Pitmaster:** Bob Palmgren **Wood:** Hickory

If you had only two choices for early Sunday morning breakfast, would you choose Kansas City barbecue, or would you rather stand in front of New York City's flagship Tiffany's on Fifth Avenue, window shopping with a to-go cup of coffee and a pastry?

You won't regret choosing a hearty sit-down country breakfast in the comfort of RJ's Bob-Be-Cue Shack on Lamar Avenue in Mission, Kansas. Served Saturday and Sunday, 8 a.m. to 1 p.m., RJ's is one of the few barbecue restaurants in Chow Town that serves real barbecue for breakfast every weekend.

Co-owners Bob & Denise Palmgren named RJ's after Bob's son, Robert Junior. They offer a delicious variety of traditional country breakfasts and some barbecue breakfasts, all served in generous portions. There are several omelet choices, fried eggs, scrambled eggs, pancakes, biscuits and gravy, smoked sausage, breakfast burritos, chicken-fried steak, country-style fried potatoes, ham, and RJ's superb house-smoked bacon, all worth your nickel.

My favorite breakfast at RJ's is the Burnt End Hash with two sunny-side up eggs, whole wheat toast, and a cup of coffee. If you want pastry, your server will bring you a frosted cinnamon roll. Instead of high-end jewelry, RJ's eye candy is a mix of John Wayne portraits; Wild West memorabilia; KU, Mizzou, Chiefs, and Royals sports logos; barbecue contest ribbons, trophies and certificates; and beer signs. The shack exudes a warm, welcoming ambience.

Besides the best barbecue breakfast in town, RJ's offers a full menu of Kansas City favorites every day of the week: pork spareribs, babyback ribs, lamb ribs, beef brisket, burnt ends, chicken, chicken wings, and fried catfish, with sides of pit beans, mac & cheese, fries, sweet potato fries, and more. Bob's creative appetizers are delicious enough to select some for your entree. I especially like the bison empanadas, Cajun crab cake, and jalapeño sausage smoked in dried corn husks.

The Shack features live music on weekends, weather permitting, in the "Mission City Limits" area out back. Bob, Denise, and staff do a great job of feeding you and making you feel welcome.

Roscoe's BBQ

9711 Kaw Dr., Edwardsville, KS 66111; (913) 422-4600; www.roscoes kcbbq.com **Founded:** 2009 **Pitmaster:** Roscoe Davis **Wood:** Hickory, apple & cherry

Their barbecue started out on high notes when Roscoe and Mariann Davis opened Roscoe's family-owned and -operated barbecue restaurant on Kaw Drive in 2009. Since then the Davis family has strived to move their bar of barbecue excellence higher every day. That's not to say that their signature lightly seasoned/kissed-with-smoke flavor profile changes dramatically. Roscoe's chicken, beef, ham, turkey, burnt ends, and ribs consistently please customers with the flavor they expect. It just always gets better.

Try the pork pie on your first visit. The pulled pork, coleslaw, slow-smoked pit beans, and Fritos corn chips combo will win you over. Like a barbecue sundae, it's a complete meal. On subsequent visits, graze your way through the entire menu. Roscoe has mastered the art of slow-smoked, lightly seasoned Kansas City–style barbecue, but he won't stop at that. And that's good.

The Rub Bar-B-Que

10512 S Ridgeview Rd., Olathe, KS 66061; (913) 894-1820; http://therubbarbque.com **Founded:** 2014 **Pitmaster:** Dan Janssen **Wood:** Hickory

Olathe was so named by founder Dr. John T. Barton and associates in 1867. They understood "olathe" to mean "beautiful" in the Shawnee language.

Olathe was founded a year ahead of Kansas statehood and more than two decades before the Model T was in mass production. It was a long ride by horse-drawn carriage from Kansas City, Kansas, and Missouri to Olathe. Today Olathe's niche in metro Kansas City's southward expansion is minutes away via modern highways.

Olathe has five excellent barbecue restaurants today. The Rub Bar-B-Que, one of the newest of Olathe's stellar lineup, features a refreshing blend of traditional and gourmet barbecue delights, thanks to the creative talents of chef/pitmaster Dan Janssen.

I asked Dan if Rub is an acronym, like Kansas City Chef Paul Kirk's former Righteous Urban Barbecue in New York City. He said no to that, as well as to ones named Rub in Chicago and Detroit, not affiliated with the Olathe restaurant. "We use Rub to refer to all the good stuff that we put on the meat," he said.

The Rub was born in 2011 when fellow competition barbecue teammates—Dave Tines, Kevin Boetcher, and Dan Janssen—decided to take a leap and give it a try. Dan's background as an experienced professional chef, combined with what he has learned as an award-winning competition pitmaster, resulted in a barbecue restaurant that hits high marks on appearance, tenderness, and flavor. It is barbecue cooked to perfection, served with an explosion of complementary flavors. I love it!

I was skeptical about the "Hillbilly Bowl." It was a given that a bowl so named would have no resemblance to the fried chicken, mashed potatoes and gravy, poke sallet, skillet cornbread, and fresh green beans from the garden feasts that Aunt Mae and Cousin Geraldine used to serve us when our family visited them in their Ozark home during my childhood. The main use we had for small bowls back then was cereal or haircuts.

My friend Gary and I agreed that our "Hillbilly Bowl," consisting of burnt ends, sugar-crusted cornbread, and pit beans, topped with crispy onion straws, was absolutely delicious. Likewise the platter of ribs, brisket, pulled pork, and burnt ends we sampled on the side, along with Kate's cheesy corn and Carolina slaw.

Today the best place to imagine the beauty that Dr. Barton saw in the original Olathe landscape is at the Prairie Center, a 300-acre oasis of native grasses, wildflowers, trees, wetlands, and wildlife near downtown Olathe. Whatever the season, you'll see "beautiful" each time you visit.

The Rub is in a strip mall on the edge of Olathe prairie. What's most beautiful there is inside in bowls and on platters.

If Dr. Barton could magically time travel to The Rub and gaze upon a Hillbilly Bowl, he would exclaim, "Beautiful!" And he would savor every bite.

Slap's BBQ

553 Central Ave., Kansas City, KS 66101; (913)-213-3736; www.facebook.com/SlapsBBQ?fref=photo **Founded:** 2014 **Pitmasters:** Joe & Mike Pearce **Wood:** Hickory & oak

Slap's, acronym for Squeal Like A Pig, started as a competition team. Their tremendous success led to positive media attention, which led to their decision to open a barbecue restaurant.

No wonder customers line up early before the doors open at 11. Slap's BBQ serves some of the best barbecue in Kansas City in a friendly, family-owned environment. Joe and Mike Pearce and their mother, Francine, work up front behind the counter; brother Jonathan works in the kitchen. Mike Pearce believes his turkey and ribs rival Aaron Franklin's in Austin, but he gives Aaron a slight edge on brisket. You can tell the Pearce brothers have done their Central Texas homework. It's almost like they see their competition as Austin, Lockhart, Luling, and Taylor instead of Joe's, Jack, Gates, and Bryant's. Ironically, they are only a few blocks away from one of Kansas City's and the region's best sausage makers, Krizman's, yet Mike told me they get their sausage from Lockhart, Texas.

Watch out, big guys. The Pearce brothers are passionate about cooking and serving top-quality barbecue fresh from the pit.

My favorite Slap's sides are the hush puppies, cheesy corn, and warm baked potato salad. Corn kernels mixed in with the hush puppies batter lend a perfect flavor kick. The puppies are especially delicious dipped in cheesy corn sauce or topped with a dab of barbecue sauce.

If they're sold out of what you wanted when you make it to Strawberry Hill to try them out, get there earlier next time. Whatever meat hasn't sold out, buy it.

Slap's is open for lunch only, from 11 a.m. until sold out.

Smoke Box Bar-B-Que

10020 N Ambassador Dr., Kansas City, MO 64153; (816) 891-8011; www.smokeboxbbq.net **Founded:** 1992 **Pitmaster:** Michael Occhipinto & smoke crew **Wood:** Hickory

Thousands of vehicles pass Smoke Box on I-29 daily. The Tiffany Springs Parkway/I-29 location puts Smoke Box within sight and smell of the major route to Kansas City business parks, industrial sites, hotels, and international airport. Granted, "international" is more hope than reality since our only international non-stop flights at present fly to cities in Mexico and Canada. Our hometown pundit, New Yorker Calvin Trillin, once mused that it's international because it's so far north that it's almost in Canada.

Smoke Box is your last chance to stop and pack some Kansas City barbecue in your check-in luggage or eat while you await your flight before going through security. Stop in and ask Michael Occhipinto or another co-owner or staffer for a carryout order of the best barbecue in the Box. My guess is he will first ask what you like. If you reply, "Surprise me," you might get a sampling of sliced brisket, pulled pork, chicken, a rib, sliced ham, burnt ends, and sausage with pit beans, cheesy corn, and your choice of regular fries or sweet potato fries.

Smoke Box is a favorite of Kansas City barbecue lovers who live near and far because the appetizers, sides, and barbecue are just darned delicious, the staff is friendly, and the ambience is upbeat.

If you or anyone in your group would rather eat something other than barbecue, Smoke Box has a lot to choose from: fried catfish sandwich, fried breaded chicken sandwich, inferno wings, fried

cheese ravioli, mozzarella cheese sticks, jalapeño poppers, cauliflower, onion rings, and a variety of salads.

Smokehouse Barbecue

7121 W 135th St., Overland Park, KS 66223; (913) 685-1717; multiple locations listed at the end; www.smokehousebbq.com **Founded:** 1990 **Pitmaster:** varies by location **Wood:** Hickory

Any barbecue establishment that has survived for more than 25 years in Kansas City and has achieved a level of success to expand beyond their original location to four others, including one in Missouri's capital city, Columbia, has to be serving barbecue and sides you can trust. As a customer who has most often enjoyed the barbecue served in Smokehouse's original Gladstone restaurant, I'm not surprised at their long-term success.

Every item on the menu has its fans. Here's what I recommend on your first visit: the Cheddar Dipped Cauliflower appetizer with ranch dip and the BBQ Combo Dinner with burnt ends and pulled pork or chicken. Although Smokehouse sauce is a good balance of sweet and sour, remember to order

your sauce on the side. That way you're in control of how much or how little will complement your delicious smoked meats. Get the hickory pit beans and house-made coleslaw sides. Pay a little extra for a third side: crispy fries or cheesy corn. Enjoy the feast. You'll be back. Next time enjoy a ribs platter. Additional locations:

Zona Rosa, 8451 NW Prairie View Rd., Kansas City, MO 64153; (816) 587-3337

6304 N Oak, Gladstone, MO 64118; (816) 454-4500

19000 E 39th St., Independence, MO 64057; (816) 795-5555

403 Stadium Blvd., Columbia, MO 65203; (573) 445-4300

Smokey's on the Blvd BBQ

14521 Metcalf Ave., Overland Park, KS 66223; (913) 897-7427; www.smokeysbbq-opks.com **Founded:** 2013 **Pitmasters:** Rob & Jason Harris **Wood:** Hickory

Tucked among other eats places and a variety of retail shops, Smokey's on the Blvd BBQ attracts a loyal following and new fans by serving consistently great barbecue with friendly service. New customers are hooked at first bite.

Some learned about Smokey's while surfing for a place they hadn't tried yet, others by word-of-mouth recommendations or just happening to spy it

and try it. Owner/operators Jason, Rob, and Mandy Harris are committed to barbecue excellence in this niche of the metro area barbecue market, and they are getting it done.

Smokey's interior is clean and comfortable with a funky tone enhanced by a large eye-catching "Lost in the '50s" mural on the dining room wall, featuring popular teen vehicles of that era.

Smokey's barbecue is as up-to-date in Kansas City today as it would have been in the '50s. It is barbecue that never goes out of style. Smokey's untrimmed Kansas City-style pork spareribs are meaty, with nice bark and a perfect kiss of smoke. Don't get Rob started on why he and Jason aren't fans of contest-style St. Louis cut ribs. Feasting on their Kansas City-style spares is explanation enough. As further proof, one lucky day when my friend Gary Bronkema and I stopped by Smokey's, Rob and Jason doubled our rib order: one set of St. Louis cut ribs and one set Kansas City style. They were cooked in the same pit, same method. We agreed that the Kansas City-style ribs were hands down superior. We also agreed that had we only been served the St. Louis cut we'd have given it high marks. After a side-by-side comparison, however, the St. Louis cut ribs didn't hold a hickory ember to the Kansas City-style ribs.

Smokey's is where I send barbecue-spaghetti-deprived current or former Memphians for a fix. It doesn't compare to the Bar-B-Q Shop in ambience and legacy, but they won't throw bones at it. Instead of spaghetti topped with pulled pork and barbecue sauce, Smokey's tops your spaghetti with beans, a choice of meat, and barbecue sauce. It is delicious.

Smokey's will serve you straight up traditional barbecue—ribs, beef, pork, turkey, ham, chicken—or barbecue in a variety of creative combinations. Besides barbecue spaghetti, the Harris family offers barbecue eggrolls, the Pig Mac homemade mac & cheese topped with pulled pork, and their signature dish, The Boulevard: a big helping of pulled pork crowned with Havarti cheese, two onion rings, and sauce. In addition to traditional sides—beans, coleslaw and fries—Smokey's has baked cheesy potatoes, sweet potato, onion rings, fried mushrooms, house salad, potato salad, mac & cheese, and fried mac & cheese.

Locals or diners on the run can call ahead and pick up their order at Smokey's drive-thru window.

When you see Jose Peppers and Sunset Grill at 145th and Metcalf, you'll find Smokey's. Step inside and feast on some great barbecue.

Smokin' Guns BBQ

1218 Swift St., North Kansas City, MO 64116; (816) 221-2535;
www.smokingunsbbq.com **Founded:** 2003 **Pitmaster:** Phil Hopkins
Wood: Mix of oak & cherry wood pellets

What's smoking here is meat, not guns. Although the name and two pistols
in the logo conjure up a Wild West scene, the ambience in this place is tame.
That's exactly the mood that lends itself to the enjoyment of barbecue as a
comfort food.

I don't know about their prowess with guns, but Phil and Linda Hopkins's prowess with smoke is remarkable, and they have the ribbons and trophies to prove it. One of their most prestigious and coveted trophies, Grand Champion, Jack Daniel's World Championship Invitational Barbecue, was awarded in 1999, giving them permanent bragging rights for achieving what few teams have accomplished. They are one of only three teams from Kansas City to win Grand Champion at The Jack.

Although you can't go wrong with any of the meats at Smokin' Guns, my favorites are the spareribs, babyback ribs, and beef burnt ends. My three favorite sides are the beans, potato casserole, and coleslaw with a vinegar base dressing, a perfect complement to the pulled pork.

Smokin' Joe's BBQ

519 E Santa Fe St., Olathe, KS 66061; (913) 780-5511; www.smokinjoes bbqolathe.com **Founded:** 1989 **Pitmaster:** Matt Sander & pit crew **Wood:** Hickory

Kansas Citians who live and/or work in Olathe have excellent barbecue options. The options have changed over the past three decades or more. Allen's is gone. Santa Fe Trail is gone. Gates is gone. One constant is the oldest Joe in town, Smokin' Joe's.

Smokin' Joe's is the nearest barbecue joint to the county courthouse and other government buildings in Johnson County, the most affluent county in Kansas. Olathe, pronounced "Oh-lay-thu," meaning "beautiful" in Shawnee Tribe language, is the county seat. It is a sprawling mix of old and new downtown residential, government, and business properties surrounded by vast suburban developments on former prairie and agricultural land. Some residents live there and work there. Many live there and work elsewhere. It's a long shot from the "little Olathe" Truman Capote described in his nonfiction crime novel, *In Cold Blood*.

Smokin' Joe's is the smallest barbecue joint in Olathe, but it holds its own in quality and customer loyalty with the other three exemplars of Kansas City barbecue excellence: Johnny's, Joe's Kansas City, and The Rub.

As with many barbecue joints in America, Smokin' Joe's building looks like a convert from a previous business, maybe tacos or pizza. Whatever the prior tenant, Smokin' Joes' has been there long enough to stake its claim. It looks like, smells like, tastes like, and is an established barbecue joint.

Not much has changed since current owner Matt Sander's brother, Ralph, opened the place in 1989. Same order/pick-up counter. Same dining arrangements, with limited dining in the order area and more dining in the adjacent wood-paneled dining room adorned with framed photos of horses, riders, and breeders, plus antique artifacts from Midwestern farm life that you might find in Great Grandma's attic or a flea market.

Matt has been the sole proprietor since 1999. He brought prior experience at Smokin' Joe's and another Kansas City barbecue restaurant before taking the leap as sole proprietor.

My favorite feast at Smokin' Joe's is and always has been the ribs, beans, fries, and slaw combo. Kissed and cooked with 100 percent hickory, these ribs are old-style Kansas City. No fancy trimming. No skinning. Just smoked to the bone tender, meaty, juicy ribs.

The beef is lean, no fat, making it dry but easy to chew, with good flavor. On the other hand, the beef burnt ends are tender, moist, and not to be missed. The pulled pork is juicy, tender, kissed with smoke, and flavorful; likewise the smoked sausage. Unlike some places, the rib tips are meaty, moist, and tender.

Smokin' Joe's is one of the few remaining barbecue joints in Kansas City that has hot pickles, no longer available at the old standard, Rosedale's. Whole hot dills are cut into spears like at Wyandot BBQ.

If nothing short of a decadent distraction from your sorrows will do, Smokin' Joe's Big Bad Joe sandwich will do the job. After you indulge with a full pound of beef, turkey, pulled pork, sausage, Pepper Jack cheese, American cheese, bacon, fries, and spicy barbecue sauce in a big bad bun, you'll be ready for a nap instead of an appointment with a lawyer, probation officer, or counselor.

With food like this, what better way to mourn or celebrate one of life's milestones? Whether you're mourning, celebrating, or simply satisfying a hunger for good barbecue, you'll be glad Smokin' Joe's got your attention.

Snead's Bar-B-Q

1001 E 171st St. (171st & Holmes), Belton, MO 64012; (816) 331-7979; www.sneadsbbq.com **Founded:** 1956 **Pitmaster:** Matt Gfeller **Wood:** Hickory

When the friendly mothers and daughters of rural Missouri put your platter of barbecue on the table, you'll know it was worth the drive to Snead's. The hickory smoked selection of meats here is fresh, tender, and delicious. Turkey, ham, pork, beef, "brownies"—Snead's jargon for burnt ends—and ribs have attracted tens of thousands of hungry customers to this hilltop barbecue beacon since the late Bill Snead opened for business in November 1956.

Some things haven't changed at the original "Snead's Corner Bar-B-Q," located on the corner of the old Snead farmstead at 171st & Holmes in Belton, Missouri. The original poured concrete building with add-on dining area and hand-built brick barbecue pit—all constructed by the late Bill Snead—is built to endure for present generations and beyond. The original pie-slice-shaped, red and white sign with a smiling pink pig sits atop a weathered white metal pole, welcoming all who hunger for good old-fashioned Kansas City barbecue.

The menu features Snead's old standbys since 1956. Prices, of course, have changed with the times. A regular ham, turkey, beef, pork, or sausage sandwich will cost you $6.99 instead of $1. A combination platter of four meats costs $20.99 instead of $3.50. "Brownies" are $10.99 for a small order instead of $1.25. Gone are the long or short end open-face rib sandwiches for $1.25, but you can get a hearty half slab rib dinner with hand-cut fries, toast, pickle, and complimentary house-made coleslaw for $14.25.

Snead's barbecue meat is smoked with 100 percent hickory in founder Bill Snead's pit. True to the late Mr. Snead's barbecue method, the meat is lightly smoke seasoned. Salt, pepper, and sauces are on each table for use as you wish. My friend, Gary, and I savored a four-meat combo platter of pulled

pork, brownies, sausage, and turkey plus a half slab of ribs with and without sauce, and found them equally delicious. The pulled pork is lightly sauced, not optional. I prefer to add seasonings if needed, but Gary and I agreed that Snead's sauce goes well with the pork. Hand-cut fries, pit beans, and coleslaw on the side were a perfect complement. Save room for Debbie Masterson's bread pudding!

The add-on dining area, built by Mr. Snead in 1972, is unlike the original Missouri walnut-paneled dining room, still functioning as a reception and dining area. It is adorned with deer heads, sans the hanging plastic plants and other country-style touches of the past.

Today's main dining room resembles a church social hall—lengthy, well-lit, beige linoleum tile on poured concrete flooring, with generic white acoustical ceiling tiles. There are new overhead fans, CFL spiral light bulbs, booth and table seating along each wall, and two rows of tables and chairs down the middle. A happy choir leader, songbook in hand, urging us to join her in a chorus of "Revive Us Again," would fit right in.

Today's servers wear black slacks and gray Snead's T-shirts instead of the dresses and aprons of yesteryear. What matters more than their attire is the food they deliver. If you're suffering from barbecue deprivation or are simply hungry for good barbecue, Snead's barbecue will revive you again, guaranteed.

Kudos to Snead's owner, Sherry Siscoe, general manager Morries T., pitmaster Matt Gfeller, cooks, kitchen staff, and servers for continuing the Snead's legacy one great meal at a time. Try Snead's and you'll understand why customers keep coming back.

The Stack Bar BQ

8920 Wornall Rd., Kansas City, MO 64114; (816) 444-7675; www.thestackbarbq.com **Founded:** 2012, opened current location, 2014 **Pitmaster:** Jeff Hallier & pit crew **Wood:** Hickory

The Stack Bar BQ was formerly known as Smokestack. New co-owners, Jeff Hallier and Heather Dukes, are continuing the legacy of Smokestack founder, the late Mary Fiorella McPheron. Jeff and Heather re-branded as The Stack Bar BQ, and although they have added their own signatures and flavors to the menu, you can still taste an important piece of Kansas City barbecue history with each bite of ribs, burnt ends, sausage, brisket, pulled pork, pit beans, coleslaw, and fries at The Stack.

Red walls accented with stretches of corrugated roofing metal along the lower portion of the walls, plus framed photos, pig art, and other memorabilia lend a relaxed, welcoming atmosphere.

Go for the specials featuring pulled pork, brisket, turkey, and ribs, with pit beans, cheesy corn, and fries. Add a serving of burnt ends. If it is too much for one meal, take home the leftovers for feasting later.

Or, if you're up to the challenge, try The Stack signature sandwich: a full half pound of tender beef brisket, American cheese, onion, lettuce, tomato, and Thousand Island dressing. I suggest ordering it cut in half to share with a friend on your first try.

Kudos to Jeff and Heather for keeping this historic Kansas City barbecue tradition alive!

Summit Hickory Pit BBQ

1012 SE Blue Pkwy., Lee's Summit, MO 64063; (816) 246-4434; www.thesummithickorypitbbq.com **Founded:** 1992 **Pitmasters:** Allen Birchfield, Danny Williams & Chris Sanders **Wood:** Hickory

Everything about Summit Hickory Pit BBQ is substantial: a big, solid, free-standing brick building; friendly staff; old-fashioned decor with vintage memorabilia in a brick and wood context; solid brick hickory fired pit; and a menu with enough variety to satisfy any appetite. No wonder it's a Lee's Summit favorite as well as a destination for metro Kansas Citians attracted to the ambience and food. Summit's barbecue menu features pork spareribs, baby-back ribs, beef brisket, burnt ends, chicken, chicken wings, ham, and pork from the pit. Grilled items include T-bone steaks, chicken breast, burgers, salmon, and catfish. There are enough tasty sides for a feast in itself: pit beans, salads, slaw, mac & cheese, cheesy potato casserole, baked potatoes, fries, baked sweet potato, sweet potato fries, potato skins, onion rings, and more. As I always suggest: Order your meat naked with sauce on the side so you can savor the natural flavors and add just enough sauce to complement. Ask your server to add a bottle of sauce to your bill for take-home, or buy some on your way out. Summit owner Katy Birchfield and staff pay attention to details: decor, cleanliness, customer satisfaction, plating, and food quality—and that is of substantial importance.

Tin Kitchen

509 Main St., Weston, MO 64098; (816) 640-0100; www.tin-kitchen
.com **Founded:** 2014 **Pitmaster:** Sean O'Malley **Wood:** Pecan
Established in 1836, Weston, Missouri, was one of the largest port cities on
the Missouri River, exceeding St. Joseph and Kansas City in population by
1850. The Lewis and Clark expedition camped there before Weston was settled. Later, young Buffalo Bill Cody and descendants of Daniel Boone lived in
Weston. Before the Missouri River changed course and made Weston land-
locked, the economy thrived as a port city. Hemp and tobacco farming also
thrived. Missouri, a slave state, did not secede from the Union during the Civil
War, but where you stood on the question of slavery or abolition was a matter
of life or death during the antebellum years.

Today's Weston, a welcoming community of fewer than 2,000 people, is
a popular destination for history buffs, shoppers in search of unique finds,
and people who love good eats and drinks. Tin Kitchen barbecue is attracting
many Kansas City tourists and barbecue lovers to the Weston culinary scene.

Sean O'Malley, formerly of O'Malley's Irish Pub, a popular historic estab-

lishment in Weston since 1976,
is Tin Kitchen's pitmaster. The
O'Malleys sold the pub in 2012
and started renovating the former
Rumpel Hardware store on Main
Street, taking pains to preserve
the historic character of the space
while making it appealing and
functional for diners. Tin Kitchen
opened in October 2014.

Thanks to Sean and his sib-
ling co-owners, Kathleen and Barbara, the former hardware store's
vintage tin ceilings are preserved
throughout the establishment.
Family patriarch Pat O'Malley is
often on the premises to mentor
and help out where needed. Tin Kitchen's barbecue sauce and 24 Hour Slaw
recipes are originals from family matriarch, the late Barbara O'Malley.

Tin Kitchen's pecan-smoked barbecue is a welcome addition to the
Weston cuisine scene. Treat yourself to a Carolina pulled pork sandwich with
ribs and hand-cut fries. Sean also offers an outstanding variety of gourmet

burgers. His Q Sandwich—beef brisket topped with cheddar cheese, onion straws, and barbecue sauce—is not to be missed.

Enjoy with iced tea, an Arnold Palmer, or a variety of craft beers. House wines also available.

The Carolina Pulled Pork Sandwich features juicy, tender pork with a perfect butt/bark ratio, kissed with mellow pecan smoke and garnished with 24 Hour Slaw, unlike any slaw I've enjoyed in North Carolina, Kansas City, or Memphis. You could call it a Weston North Carolina Pulled Pork Sandwich. We called it superb.

The neatly trimmed St. Louis–/contest-style pork ribs are perfectly tender, smoked to the bone with a sweet glaze and rub hinting of chili seasoning similar to Memphis's Rendezvous.

The baked beans are something different. Your spoon or fork will stand upright in these beans. Bean lovers and bean counters savor Tin Kitchen's thick combo of kidney, pinto, and prepared white beans, baked with a mix of brisket, pulled pork, and barbecue sauce: different and delicious.

Mrs. O'Malley's thick, tomatoey barbecue sauce with herbal/molasses accents and a sweet/sour balance doesn't promise much when tasted alone. Put a small amount on any barbecue meat, however, and it comes to life as an excellent complement.

Sean O'Malley's pitmaster mentor, barbecue legend Mike Mills, taught him well. What Sean is producing with his Ole Hickory pecan-fueled pit is good enough to make Jayhawkers whistle Dixie, and so are the sides.

Cigar aficionados: Don't miss visiting with Corey Frisbee, proprietor of Weston Tobacco Company, down the street from Tin Kitchen. He hand rolls and sells quality cigars and a variety of related products directly below a historic tobacco auction barn.

Wabash BBQ & Blues Garden – the original

646 Kansas City Ave. S, Excelsior Springs, MO 64024; (816) 630-7700; second location at 1 Elm St., Chillicothe, MO 64601; (660) 646-6777; www.wabashbbq.com **Pitmasters:** Mitch Dickey & pit crew **Wood:** Hickory & apple

Hobos who rode the rails from one city to another in search of work during the hard economic times of the 1930s imagined that their final ride, into the hereafter, would be on the mythical "Wabash Cannonball."

Mythical "death train" aside, there really was a Wabash Railway Station that served for a few years as a branch line linking passengers from Excelsior Springs to major rails to St. Louis and beyond. In 1933 the Wabash rails and

station were closed. Travel to St. Louis by bus or private auto on improved highways drastically reduced customer demand for the Wabash line.

When the prized, solidly built brick Wabash station with immaculate landscaping was no longer needed for its original purpose, it was temporarily abandoned until local dairy farmer Leonard Johnson bought it. The Johnson family converted the station building into an ice cream, soda, and burger shop with an add-on room for dairy operations. Eventually the shakes, ice cream, coffee, soda, and burger business was shuttered to make more room for expanded dairy operations. Later the building and dairy business was owned and operated by the Mid America Dairy Association. After they vacated the building in 1985, it was converted to a printing business until the building was sold to the current co-owners, Jim and Cheri McCullough, with Mitch and

Malinda Dickey. Cheri and Mitch, Kauffman Foundation Entrepreneurial All Star award winners, run daily operations in both Wabash BBQ restaurants.

Thanks to the McCullough and Dickey families, the old Wabash station is realizing its true destiny. Wabash BBQ is there to sustain us. All myths aside, Wabash authentic hickory-smoked barbecue is food for the gods!

Wabash BBQ is ideally located in Excelsior Springs, a community long known for the restorative powers of its natural mineral waters—waters so significant to the locale that city hall itself is dubbed Hall of Waters.

The Wabash BBQ property sports three buildings. Behind the restaurant is a large smokehouse with two chimneys pumping out hickory smoke from the meat fires inside. Up the hill a ways is the ice house bar and a stage where live blues performances happen during Missouri shirtsleeve months. Other than B.B.'s Lawnside and Knuckleheads, this is one of the few places in metro Kansas City that you can occasionally get live blues with your barbecue.

A step inside the non-smoking dining room in the original building is a step into Midwestern agribusiness history. The architecture is unchanged. Old signs, memorabilia, and framed posters from the American Royal Barbecue adorn the walls. The adjacent barroom echoes the old-time historic feel. The south side dining room, with a separate entrance, was originally added on when the former dairy company needed more space to expand operations. It has a modern red brick feel. Regardless of where you dine at Wabash, the barbecue is the same and you are in for a treat.

The best entree to try on your first visit is the Piggyback Combo with an add-on order of burnt ends. If you're solo you'll have take-home leftovers; otherwise, two to four can graze on this combo with ease. Sliced beef brisket, turkey, ham, sliced pork, ribs, and burnt ends deliver the full Wabash barbecue flavor profile: distinctly different meat flavors, each kissed with smoke and complementary seasonings. With or without the Wabash lightly seasoned smooth tomato base sauce, it is all delicious. The combo comes with two sides. I especially like Wabash fries and beans.

Wabash "Conductor's Favorites" sandwiches are a big hit with customers. Each is named with railroad jargon: Iron Horse, Roundhouse, Depot, Wabash, Golden Spike, and Steamer. All except the Train Track Tenderloin feature single or multiple portions of barbecue. As a fan of barbecue baloney I wish Cheri and Mitch would add a smoked baloney sandwich with raw onions and dill chips to the menu. Call it the Gandy Dancer in honor of the working class railroad workers who kept the rails safe for travel.

Excelsior Springs has enjoyed a longtime reputation as a place to go for R&R. Rolling hills, bluffs, hardwood forests, and the restorative powers of natural mineral waters have attracted tourists and metro Kansas Citians hungry for weekend romantic or family getaways at the Elms Hotel & Spa for more than a century. When Wabash BBQ opened in 1997, a short distance across Kansas City Avenue S from the Elms, Excelsior Springs added a new compelling reason to come visit and be restored. As the Wabash slogan asserts, they are "Always Smokin' Something Good."

Forget the plane. Forget the train. Go to Wabash BBQ by car. Your Wabash Cannonball can wait. Go feast!

We B Smokin BBQ

32580 Airport Rd., Paola, KS 66071; (913) 256-6802; http://websmok in.com **Founded:** 2001 **Pitmaster:** Brian & Terry Bright **Wood:** Apple & cherry

How many of the more than 40,000 airports on the planet feature a genuine family-owned, stick-burner barbecue restaurant? The jury is still out, but my guess is there are no more than you can count on one hand—maybe even just one finger. When you arrive by small plane, helicopter, or auto at the Miami (pronounced "My-am-uh") County Airport between Paola and Osawatomie, Kansas, you've found it.

Several barbecue joints around the country are located near small airports, especially in North Carolina. Several metropolitan airports have a barbecue venue of one kind or another, usually with barbecue supplied from the

home base commissary. Memphis, Nashville, Atlanta, Austin-Bergstrom, and Houston come to mind. Few airports, however, have a genuine barbecue joint in the airport terminal with easy access after landing. We B Smokin is that kind of barbecue joint.

Founders/co-owners, Terry and Gloria Bright, brought prior restaurant experience plus successful competition barbecue skills to the business when they decided to sign the lease and launch what has become a phenomenon in Kansas and beyond. Bobby Flay found it in 2004. President Barack Obama found it in 2011.

But a barbecue joint can't survive on visits from occasional celebrities alone. To make it as a business you have to attract a steady base of customers, new and repeat. The Bright family is doing just that, with about 30 percent of their business from small aircraft pilots and 70 percent from a mix of bikers, workers, businesspeople, farmers, and tourists. Terry and Gloria's children, spouses, and grandchildren are also big fans.

Terry was pitmaster for years. Now their son Brian does the honors, with Terry pitching in now and then. They keep their big stick burner with offset firebox filled to capacity with brisket, chicken, spareribs, babybacks, and pork. They mostly smoke with apple and wild cherry. Their specialty is We-B Sticky Ribs: a full slab of smoked babybacks sprinkled with honey and barbecue sauce. That explains their motto, "Where sticky fingers are a good thing."

My favorites are the spareribs, beef, and pork with fries and beans. The beans remind me of New England-style bean hole beans, due to the maple syrup sweetness—except these beans are better. They are so good, in fact, that Gloria and Terry said most of the pilots love them and one loves them so much that he flies in from time to time just to eat the beans.

We B Smokin is seriously good barbecue in a fun, small airport terminal atmosphere. It is worth going out of your way to enjoy it.

Werner's Fine Sausages

5736 Johnson Dr., Mission, KS 66202; (913) 362-5955; http://werners wurst.com **Founded:** 1974 **Pitmaster:** David Miller Grillmasters: Tom Roth & Rachel Cochran **Wood:** Hickory

Although Werner's is not a barbecue joint per se, its barbecue pedigree is as old as commercial barbecue's budding in this city in the late 19th and early 20th centuries.

Werner's is a Kansas City favorite go-to place for hickory-smoked meats and fresh meats and sausages for outdoor and indoor cooks. Originally on Westport Road on the Missouri side of the metro area in 1898, it was known as

Swanson's, a Swedish deli and meat market. When Werner Wohlert bought Swanson's in 1972 after working there for many years, he changed the name to Werner's and moved it to Mission, Kansas, in 1974, closer to a larger population of Kansas Citians of German descent. David and Judy Miller kept the name when they bought the store from Werner in 1995.

Werner's is known as a go-to place for quality meats. No wonder. Werner's has always been staffed by trained, skilled butchers. Werner was an apprenticed butcher in Germany when he moved to Kansas City and worked at Swanson's. David Miller is a trained, skilled butcher.

Weekday and Saturday customers flock to Werner's for lunchtime sandwiches, either carrying them out, or eating them while sitting on stools at the streetside counter. Saturdays are especially popular. Weather permitting, hundreds of customers since the 1990s have lined up for Werner's flame-grilled brats and other sausages on a bun, with beans, potato salad, or potato chips on the side. The magic touch of former grillmaster Steve Brunner has been channeled to today's expert grillmasters Tom Roth and Rachel Cochran. They are so good they can make a grilled brat or knockwurst rival the wow power of a Kansas City strip.

Dave Miller has expanded the variety of handmade sausages in Werner's repertoire over the years in response to customer demand. "I wish you had bangers," a customer who moved to Kansas City from London remarked one day. Dave replied, "Get me a recipe and I'll make them." Soon he was on the phone with the lady's former butcher in London, discussing ingredients and method. She loved the result and so do others, as bangers are a popular item at Werner's. Current selections besides traditional bratwurst and bangers include Norwegian potato sausage, Lithuanian desros sausage, Mexican chorizo, Cajun andouille, knackwurst, cheddar bier brat, Polish, Italian (mild and firecracker), linguica (andouille/chorizo mix), breakfast sausage, and more. Werner's has become a United Nations of Sausage.

Knowing the importance of passing recipes and know-how from one generation to the next, Dave has trained Bernie Gumpert as Werner's official sausage master.

Winslow's BBQ

20 E Fifth St., Kansas City, MO 64106; (816) 471-4727; www.winslows bbq.com **Founded:** 1971 **Pitmaster:** Gerry Heldrich & pit crew **Wood:** Hickory

The late Don Winslow, known as Kansas City's "Sultan of Smoke" in the 1970s, would be proud that his footprint and legacy in this smokehouse he made famous is still thriving. Winslow and his mother, Addie, opened Winslow's BBQ in 1972 in the same City Market location where you'll find it today.

After Don's untimely death in the early 1990s, his brother David took over. David sold Winslow's to a friend, Gerry Heldrich, in 2009. Fortunately the one constant through these changes has been the same quality of barbecue, from the original pit, that attracted customers to Don's barbecue since the beginning.

The brisket, turkey, ribs, and pulled pork are tender, sometimes with only a hint of smoke and a bit dry. Winslow's burnt ends are some of the most authentic and delicious of the genre that you'll find in Kansas City—tender, kissed with smoke, with some crunchy bark.

The seasoned fries and creamy coleslaw are my favorite sides. Of the two, the creamy coleslaw is mandatory. Made with real cream and fresh produce from City Market vendors, it exemplifies "Buy Fresh, Buy Local."

Winslow's barbecue is smoked in the same custom built all-wood pit that the Sultan used. If pits could talk, this one could share many fascinating stories. If the barbecue renders you speechless, however, no problem. Enjoy in silence and pass the sauce.

Barbecue belongs in City Market. Here the tradition of bartering and selling fish, fowl, and produce, fresh from the rivers, barnyards, ranches, and fields of America's Heartland, is still thriving. It is fitting that vendors and buyers have a great place to eat barbecue and socialize with each other at Winslow's BBQ, originally branded as Winslow's City Market Smokehouse. The market is now known as Kansas City River Market.

Although Winslow's has been remodeled and added on since the Sultan was smoking, a step inside still feels like a step into the smokehouse past of the 1950s, when brick and wood was the prevailing motif. Picnic tables and benches have been replaced with indoor tables and booths. The ambience, then and now, feels warm, welcoming and comfortable.

The usual variety of barbecue is on the Winslow's menu: ribs, beef brisket, burnt ends, chicken, ham, pulled pork, sausage, and turkey. They also offer jumbo smoked wings, fried pickles, and fried green beans—less common in Kansas City barbecue joints. Other sides include a delicious house-made creamy coleslaw, pit beans, sweet potato fries, regular fries, and smoked corn on the cob.

Gerry brings his own style of creative culinary magic to Winslow's. One of his standout sandwiches, an occasional special on the menu, is the bourbon bacon brisket sandwich—lean beef with a bourbon-laced kiss of smoke. It is a big hit with customers for taste and value. There should be a petition to make this a regular menu item!

Winslow's signature sauce perfectly complements the meat. The vinegar and spices work well with the molasses and tomato sauce. When Gerry is experimenting with new sauce flavors—maple/apple for example—don't hesitate to give them a try and let him know what you think. I like to think that Dave channels Don Winslow's creative spirit when he feels inspired to experiment with new flavors and menu items.

Thanks to Gerry Heldrich, the Winslow legacy in Kansas City's City Market is alive and thriving. The Sultan of Smoke would be proud!

Woodyard Bar-B-Que

3001 Merriam Ln., Kansas City, KS 66106; (913) 553-1661; (913) 362-8000; http://woodyardbbq.com **Founded:** 2007 **Pitmaster:** Mark O'Bryan **Wood:** Apple, cherry & a variety of hardwoods

Instead of being born of a successful run in competition barbecue or starting out as a restaurant, Woodyard started as a wood yard. Frank Schloegel's family has sold wood to backyard barbecue pitmasters and barbecue restaurants for decades. Stories vary as to why and when Woodyard barbecue for sale entered the picture. When I first heard about it, a neighbor told me that every Saturday the folks at Woodyard were smoking great ribs and selling slabs first come, first served until sold out. Word spread quickly. Soon co-owners Frank Schloegel and Joe Daly decided to go full-smoke ahead and add a sit-down and carryout barbecue restaurant to the site. From the original indoor dining at a few tables in the old house that serves as Woodyard's home base, demand for their barbecue has escalated to the point that they had to add expanded dining and beer garden space on portions of the former wood lot. They have also added a dining patio in front of the house.

Besides the usual ribs, chicken, brisket, sausage, and pork butt, Woodyard offers specials each day, depending on the season and whatever they decide

to feature. A local favorite is the Burnt End Chili when cold weather hits the metro area.

The hand-painted signs on weathered fence planks and scrap lumber add a note of barbecue joint authenticity to the scene.

I have savored the barbecue meats from Woodyard's pit many times over the years. They hit all the notes on your palate, even if you're a vegetarian (try the smoked veggie burger), or almost vegetarian (treat yourself to smoked salmon). It's all good, but what I like most are the Smoked Jumbo Hot Wings and the Burnt End Chili (in season). Sides of baked beans and potato salad are good with the wings.

Woodyard's sauce is respectable, mild or hot, but the meat stands admirably without sauce. Go gentle with the sauce if you do use it.

Wyandot BBQ

8441 State Ave., Kansas City, KS 66112; (913) 788-7554; second location at 7215 W 75th St., Overland Park, KS 66204; (913) 341-0609; http://wyandotbbq.com **Founded:** 1977 **Pitmaster:** Ron Williams & pit crews **Wood:** Hickory

There's nothing slick or fancy about Wyandot #1 on State Avenue. Same can be said of Wyandot #2, although the buildings are different inside and out. The barbecue inside is what's important.

In both places you order, pay, and pick up at the counter when your order is ready. When you stand at the counter to order at Wyandot #1, look up to your right at the signed framed photo of famous hometown actor and loyal customer Eric Stonestreet, best known these days as Cameron Tucker in the hit TV sitcom, *Modern Family*. "Ronnie—Ham & a fry. Best Wishes, Eric Stonestreet."

Owner/pitmaster Ron Williams learned the barbecue method of cooking and the ropes of running a barbecue business from the legendary Anthony Rieke. Ron learned it well. The business has been serving a steady line of loyal and new customers for almost forty years. Wyandot's second generation, Ron Williams II, is already an integral part of the business.

Wyandot's traditional Kansas City-style barbecue ribs and beef are my favorites. The untrimmed, unskinned hickory smoked ribs, Wyandot's

specialty, are fall-off-the-bone tender and kissed with smoke. The marriage of rib meat with rendered fat and a touch of sauce makes you wonder why Ron would bother to smoke anything else.

Kansas City barbecue customers, however, expect more than ribs on the menu. Beef, ham, turkey, sausage, and burnt ends better be on the menu. Wyandot's menu has it all. The beef is lean, tender, and smoky. No big deal that it doesn't have smoke rings. You taste the smoke, and it's just right. When Wyandot burnt ends and rib tips are fresh from the pit, they are juicy and melt-in-your-mouth tender.

Although I tend to stick with ribs, beef, beans, and fries at Wyandot, one of these days I'll try Eric's "ham and a fry." I am not a big fan of ham in most barbecue joints, mainly because it is usually cured ham warmed in a barbecue pit. I don't know of any place in Kansas City that serves ham that starts out fresh, uncured, and then smoked slow and low like the late Grace Proffitt did it at her Ridgewood Barbecue in Bluff City, Tennessee. Grace's ham barbecue and sauce legacy continues today through her son, Larry, and his daughter,

Lisa Peters. The flavor is entirely different than pit-heated, smoke-cured ham. I think it could displace smoke-cured ham as Eric's favorite.

Ron's sauce is of the Rosedale genre, but he has made it his own: tomato catsup and paste base, smooth, slightly spicy with a cayenne bite, a touch of sour and sweet, fused with that elusive Rosedale hint of cinnamon or allspice.

Zarda Bar-B-Q

11931 W 87th Street Pkwy., Lenexa, KS 66215; (913) 492-2330; second location at 214 N 7 Hwy., Blue Springs, MO 64014; (816) 229-9999; http://zarda.com **Founded:** 1979 **Pitmaster:** pit crews at each location **Wood:** Hickory

Zarda is a noun, not an acronym. It's a family name with a culinary pedigree that goes at least as far back as Norb Zarda's former hamburger stand on Highway 7 in Blue Springs, Missouri. In 1976, the first Zarda Bar-B-Q opened at the former hamburger stand location, with a new building and a cinder block

barbecue pit. The Blue Springs restaurant has since moved to a newer, larger facility, still on Highway 7. Following population growth on the other side of the metro state line, a second Zarda Bar-B-Q has been serving grateful barbecue lovers since 1979.

Zarda Bar-B-Q, at the sign of the pig in flames wafting a frosty beer mug, needs no introduction to Kansas Citians. Zarda's many fans will tell you that it's at the end of the roster because Zarda's is the closer, the last word in Kansas City barbecue. I won't argue with that.

On the outside, the Zarda family leaves no doubt that this establishment uses hickory for smoke and fire. It is stacked right out front where you can see it. Zarda's freestanding, red-roofed brick and shingles building needs no red carpet to signal that this is the place where Kansas City barbecue lovers chow down on their favorite barbecue. Zarda's menu features beef, pork, sausage, chicken, burnt ends, sausage, spareribs, beans, fries, and cheesy corn, served as dinners or in a variety of sandwiches.

Zarda is big inside. It has to be to accommodate their large customer base. The interior design, however, evokes a cozy feeling instead of the feel of a large mess hall. The decor, with real wood walls, mounted longhorns, and subdued lighting, also helps generate a warm, friendly ambience.

My Zarda favorites are the beef and pork combo sandwich, the burnt ends, and the ribs. Throw in Zarda's excellent and vastly popular pit beans with an order of onion rings, with a puddle of Zarda sauce for dipping, and let's not talk until our plates are clean.

BBQ Food Trucks

Kansas City is of course no stranger to barbecue on wheels. Food trucks have made our scene for several decades. Names and locations change. They are truly a moveable feast, but barbecue food trucks are here to stay.

Some, like Local Pig's Pigwich, are installed in a permanent location. Most are mobile. They stick to somewhat regular schedules with a steady customer base, while keeping flexibility for special events where hungry crowds gather, and for catering.

Thus far I haven't seen any Rolling Ribbers, Squeals on Wheels, Beef Relief, Butts on the Go, Pulling Pork, or BBQ 2 You, but here are a few you may be lucky enough to try.

Back Rack Food Truck & Catering

110 E 18th Ave., North Kansas City, MO 64116; (816) 565-0481; http://www.backrackbbq.com
Kansas City barbecue lovers are passionate about the local beer brewed at Cinder Block Brewery. When Cinder Block's Back Rack Food Truck is open, passions escalate with servings tender, hickory and pecan slow smoked barbecue and sides.

Crazy Good Eats

16695A W. 151st St., Olathe, KS 66062; (913) 905-2744; www.crazygood
eats.com
Complete menu of barbecue meats and sides, plus the famous Mad Meatballs. Now serving barbecue in their new restaurant, at the former Big Bubba's site, 16695A W 151st St.

ChickHoovenSwine BBQ

Based in Spring Hill, KS; (913) 636-7607; www.bbqrules.com
Serving ribs, pulled pork, brisket, smoked sausage, signature sandwiches, and barbecue nachos topped with pork or brisket, and sides made from scratch. Eric Westervelt, chef/owner

Jazzy B's BBQ Mobile Food Truck

(816) 651-5681
Serving brisket tacos, armadillo eggs, portabellas, smoked fried chicken, and other meats and sides. Catering available.

KC BBQ Truck

Based in Liberty, MO; (816) 810-2690; www.kcbbqtruck.com
Smoked ribs, pulled pork, brisket, hot links, specialty items, and secret recipe side dishes.

Quicks on Wheels

Based in Kansas City, KS; (913) 236-7228; www.quicksbbq.com; @quicksonwheels
Famous hickory-smoked barbecue from Earl Quick's pit to you. Catering available.

Werner's on Wheels

Based in Mission, KS; (913) 313-2027
Esteemed master sausage maker Dave Miller's gourmet sausage repertoire is available grilled and ready to eat from Werner's on Wheels.

Kansas City–Style Recipes for Home Cooks

Barbecue isn't rocket science. At its simplest it is a marriage of fire, smoke, and meat. Ground meat and tender cuts such as beef steaks or pork chops take well to hot and fast grilling over direct flames. Larger, tougher cuts of meat are transformed into juicy, tender deliciousness when smoked at low temperatures for hours instead of minutes.

Kansas City's four basic food groups are pork ribs, beef brisket, pork shoulder, and chicken.

Thus, this chapter begins with how to prepare and barbecue those four meats at home. There are many great variations and departures from the four basics below. Diverse recipes and opinions are hallmarks of our Kansas City style.

The basic four pay tribute to Kansas City's barbecue past, when local pitmasters bought cheap or discarded packinghouse meats and transformed them into tender, flavorful feasts of barbecue excellence. Nothing fancy, but as my friend, pitmaster Washington Perry in Sarasota, Florida, says of his barbecue, it had "the love in it."

In their drive to win trophies and cash prizes, most competition pitmasters buy the best quality meat they can afford. Besides pepper and salt, a variety of other dry and wet seasonings are used. The recipes are carefully guarded team secrets. I have no argument with buying high-quality meats and developing secret recipes, since the goal is to get an edge on the competition. That is not, however, true to the roots of original Kansas City–style barbecue. Respecting our traditional roots, I recommend getting the cheapest, toughest cuts of pork spareribs, beef brisket, and pork shoulder available. With chicken I make an exception: fryers, roasters, or broilers will yield better barbecue than older, tougher stewers.

Two popular cuts of barbecue meat in Kansas City are rib tips and burnt ends. For rib tips, smoke the meat scraps from the breast bone when you trim a slab St. Louis style. Burnt ends are so popular that most served in barbecue restaurants are cubed pieces of beef brisket, usually from the brisket flat, although some pitmasters cube entire briskets to keep up with demand for burnt ends.

Beans and potatoes are mandatory sides in Kansas City. The bean recipe in this chapter will serve you well as a good base for developing your own signature barbecue beans recipe. Several fantastic potato recipes are featured, plus another mandatory side: coleslaw.

Cheesy dishes have become so popular in Kansas City that almost every barbecue joint has a cheesy recipe or two. Some of the best are featured in this chapter.

I seldom leave room for dessert when I eat barbecue. Those who do make room for dessert will not go wanting in this chapter. Danny Edwards gives you his delicious bread pudding and apple pie recipes. Shannon "Firebug" Kimball's grilled peaches with port wine sauce is a crowd pleaser. When you crave an over-the-top sweet tooth indulgence, dig in to Chef Jeremy Tawney's Velvet Elvis!

The Classics
JOHNNY WHITE'S KANSAS CITY–STYLE RIBS

Since the advent of sanctioned barbecue competitions in Kansas City and beyond, pork spareribs have taken on a new look, as described in the KCBS Basic Four section. You can still find traditional cuts of what is commonly labeled "Kansas City Style" ribs, however, in a few Kansas City barbecue restaurants. Johnny's is one of my favorites. I asked Johnny White for the basics on how he preps and cooks his Kansas City–style ribs. Here's some of what he shared with me, adapted for home cooking.

What you need:
2 slabs untrimmed pork spareribs, about 8 pounds each, raw

About 4 ounces dry barbecue seasoning (your favorite brand or homestyle recipe)

Hickory chips, chunks, pellets, or sticks

Grill and fire source: Charcoal briquettes, gas, or all wood

Unlike the neatly trimmed rectangular "St. Louis cut," traditional Kansas City ribs are untrimmed slabs of pork spareribs. The breast bone and brisket flap are left intact and the membrane on the bony side is not removed. The shape is sort of like a lopsided, stretched out triangle instead of a rectangle.

Most ribs these days are sold wrapped in Cryovac. While your smoker fires up, put disposable food handler gloves on and remove the ribs from the Cryovac. Discard the Cryovac and place the ribs on a clean table.

Lightly sprinkle all surfaces of the ribs with dry seasoning.

When your grill is fired up to 250°F and hickory is smoking, put the ribs in, either flat, upright in a rib rack, or hanging on a hook, depending upon your type of grill.

Smoke the ribs at 225–250°F for 4½ –5 hours until tender and ready to eat.

Lightly slather the ribs with your favorite tomato base barbecue sauce before serving.

Eat and enjoy. If they are tender enough to fall of the bone, so much the better. Contest officials consider fall-off-the-bone ribs to be overcooked, but many barbecue fans want them that way. When you're in business to sell barbecue, you'd best listen to what the customer wants.

KANSAS CITY–STYLE CONTEST RIBS

True Kansas City style ribs are untrimmed pork spareribs. Due to the influence of barbecue contest judging standards and an emphasis on presentation, most Kansas City barbecue joints today trim their ribs "St. Louis style," breast bone removed, slab trimmed to rectangular shape, membrane on the bony side removed. Here we're smoking untrimmed spareribs straight out of the Cryovac packing.

Instead of a fancy mix of dry seasonings with secret or standard ingredients, let's simply sprinkle all of the meat surfaces with black pepper, followed by a light sprinkling of salt. Do this before you light your pit fire and let the rib meat soak up the seasoning while your pit fire warms up to 250°F.

I like to use a 21½-inch kettle-style grill for backyard cooking. Adapt these instructions to your own favorite grill.

What is a Rib Sandwich?

A long time ago I bought my first rib sandwich from a barbecue food truck vendor in downtown Topeka. To my surprise, I was handed a three-bone, sauced mini-slab between two slices of sandwich bread.

Once I got past my astonishment, I pulled the meat off the bones and enjoyed the sandwich.

Later I was embarrassed to learn that a rib sandwich is exactly what that food truck pitmaster gave me.

The most plausible explanation I've found is that sandwich bread is served with the ribs to soak up meat grease and sauce. Makes sense to me!

The old-time street corner Kansas City barbecue vendors most likely used homemade 55-gallon drum grills. Most early restaurants used custom-made brick pits with bars and hooks for hanging ribs to smoke.

Position your hot coals on one side of the grill, leaving enough space opposite the coals for the meat so it won't be exposed to direct heat.

When your fire is ready, place the ribs opposite the fire, either bone side down on the grill or upright horizontally in a metal rib rack.

Dump the moist, drained wood chips directly atop the coals, lid the grill and smoke the ribs at 225–245°F for 4–6 hours until tender. Pull a rib off one end of a slab to test for tenderness.

Serve as-is, or lightly slather with your favorite Kansas City–style barbecue sauce, trim off the breast bone, slice each slab into individual bones, and serve.

Contest experts will tell you that if the meat falls off the bone, you've over-cooked it. That's okay for contests, but many pitmaster/owners at barbecue joints have told me that their customers demand and expect ribs that fall off the bone. When you're in the barbecue business to make a living, you listen to your customers. When I judge ribs in a contest, I respect the rules and take off a point or two when ribs fall of the bone instead of yield from the bone with a gentle tug. When I eat at a barbecue joint or at a backyard barbecue, I have no problem with ribs so tender that they fall off the bone.

KANSAS CITY–STYLE BEEF BRISKET

Beef brisket is breast meat located at the front of the bull, steer, or cow. It consists of tough muscle and fat. Although barbecuers were once challenged to find out how to smoke brisket until tender, housewives mastered the technique years ago by roasting it for hours in a medium heat oven. Here's what I use:

Cooker – a 22-inch Weber kettle

Fire – Kingsford Charcoal Briquettes (have at least an 18-pound bag at hand)

Chimney Starter

2 cups pecan chips with 2 cups apple chips. (This combination yields a mellow smoke flavor in the brisket. Some cooks prefer oak, hickory, cherry, alder, sweet maple, mesquite, or other woods. Avoid using pine or cedar—too much resin. If you use mesquite, go easy, as it yields a stronger flavor than other woods and it burns hotter.)

1 whole (12-pound or more) untrimmed packer-cut brisket in Cryovac. Use a sharp knife to trim fat portions, leaving about ½ inch of fat. (I get the cheapest available. Contest cooks usually get prime grade to get a leg up on the competition. I've never been disappointed with the cheaper grade. Untrimmed is important. You need the fat for a tender brisket.)

Rub – optional. (If you choose to rub, try two parts pepper to one part salt on all surfaces of the meat, either overnight or shortly before the brisket goes in

The Butcher & the Lawyer

I found the original version of this story in the *New England Yankee Cookbook* by Imogene Wolcott, published in 1939. Here's my updated retelling, adapted to the Kansas City meat market scene.

> *A few years ago in Kansas City, Kansas, a lawyer's dog sneaked into Bichelmeyer Meats, sped behind the meat counter, grabbed a 12-pound brisket, and raced out the door.*
>
> *Later a regular customer, a lawyer named Hal, walked in. The butcher on duty said, "Hal, if a dog stole a brisket from our display case, could we collect from the owner of the dog?"*
>
> *"Certainly," Hal replied. "Just go to the owner and tell him. He should be glad to pay you for his dog's theft of your brisket."*
>
> *"Thank you," replied the butcher. "You owe me $60. It was your dog."*
>
> *"Well," said Hal, "the legal advice I just gave you is worth $70, so you owe me $10."*

Footnote, compliments of barbecue aficionado Michael Gross, New York City: Hal forgot to have the butcher sign a retainer before dispensing advice. Hal owes the butcher $60, no question!

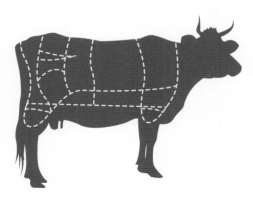

the pit. Avoid seasoning so heavily that you overpower the natural flavor of the meat.)

A 12-pound brisket will take as long as 15–18 hours, at a temperature of 225–250°F. The rule of thumb is 1½ hours per pound in Kansas City year round, allowing for a bit more time in cold weather. In higher altitudes allow for longer cooking times.

Patience with the process and waiting until the right moment to take the brisket out of the cooker will be rewarded.

COOKING THE BRISKET

Fire up a full chimney of charcoal briquettes. When they are gray, dump them on the coal grate to one side of the grill. Place the clean, oiled cooking grate in the cooker. Place the brisket fat side up, opposite the coals. Dump soaked and drained wood chips directly on the coals. This is easiest with hinged grates; otherwise you'll need to lift the grate, dump the chips on the coals, and return the grate to the pit.

Lid the cooker immediately. Monitor temperature with a built-in thermometer or put a candy thermometer in the lid vent. Control air to coals using bottom vents. My grill will go a minimum of 4 hours before more hot coals are needed.

Some cooks wrap the brisket in aluminum foil after 6–8 hours and leave it in foil for the duration. This is known as the "Texas Crutch." Some say this method yields "pot roast." The debate is never-ending. I get great results without using aluminum foil.

When the internal temperature of the brisket reaches 165°F, it's done. Use a good meat thermometer stuck into the thickest part of the meat—or, after you have smoked many briskets, you can tell it is done by feel.

Trim the excess fat before slicing the meat. Cut the meat against the grain. Pay heed to the three sets of muscles, finding the grain in each. Texans like thick slices. Kansas Citians like them thinner.

If your brisket is tender and flavorful, congratulations. You have mastered one of the most difficult cuts of meat to barbecue.

BASIC BBQ PORK SHOULDER

Longtime favorite in eastern North Carolina, barbecue pork shoulder, pulled or chopped, has enjoyed a surge of nationwide popularity in recent years, Kansas City included. Pork has always been available in Kansas City barbecue joints, but more often than not it was sliced instead of pulled or chopped. Calling the shoulder a "butt," as in the upper part of the shoulder known as a "Boston Butt," has become popular in the barbecue contest network. Many competition barbecue teams have put "butt" to creative uses in their team names.

Here's an easy way to smoke your own and enjoy the feast.

Serves 6–8

1 (8- to 10-pound) pork shoulder, bone in
Yellow prepared mustard or 12 ounces of Italian vinaigrette salad dressing
   (optional)
Pepper
Salt
Charcoal briquettes
2 cups hickory chips soaked in water for at least 30 minutes and drained

Some cooks put the shoulder in a sealable plastic bag, pour a bottle of Italian vinaigrette dressing in the bag, coat the shoulder with dressing, and let it sit overnight in the refrigerator for extra flavor. Others prefer to slather all surfaces of the shoulder with mustard before applying dry seasonings.

When your fire is ready, place the shoulder on the grill opposite the fire, put drained hickory chips on the coals, lid the grill, and smoke at 150–225°F for 10–12 hours until pull-apart tender. Pitmasters strive for meat so tender that the shoulder bone is easy to pull out.

Pork Butt Flavoring Tip

Fat Charlie showed me a little trick he has with pork butt. He adds an undisclosed amount of grease to an undisclosed amount of smoked pulled pork butt and tosses it by hand to mix in the bacon flavor. It works; darned good!

—Jay "The Snail" Vantuyl

Contest cooks during onsite judging at Memphis in May are skilled at pulling out the shoulder bone, followed by pulling out a mini-round long piece of meat known in contest circles as the "money muscle" because its flavor and tenderness resonate positively with judges.

Serve as a Carolina-style sandwich with coleslaw atop the meat, or as a meat entree with your favorite sides.

BASIC KANSAS CITY–STYLE BBQ WHOLE CHICKEN

When competing in the chicken, also known as "yard bird," contest category, most teams cook thighs instead of the whole chicken. Thighs trim nicely for eye appeal, are tender, juicy, and flavorful, and the required minimum of six or more pieces fits easily in a contest entry box. Thighs are delicious, but why not enjoy all parts of the bird? Here's an easy way to barbecue a chicken. **Serves 4–6**

1 whole (5- to 6-pound) chicken, dressed
Salt and pepper or your favorite rub
Charcoal briquettes
1 cup hickory, pecan, or apple wood chips, soaked in water for at least 30
   minutes and drained
1 (12- or 16-ounce) can beer or soda
Barbecue sauce for dipping

Rinse the chicken under cold water. Pat dry and sprinkle lightly with pepper and salt or rub.

When the coals are ready, place them on one side of your grill; put the clean, oiled grate in the grill. Open the beverage can and insert it, bottom side down, far enough inside the chicken cavity to help stabilize the chicken in an upright position.

Drop the wood chips on the coals, lid the grill, and smoke the chicken at 150–225°F for 2–2½ hours until done and tender.

Let the meat rest for 30–40 minutes before carving. Serve with a sweet Kansas City–style tomato base barbecue sauce on the side for dipping.

Notes: Chicken should reach an internal temperature of 160°F. If juices are pink, the chicken isn't fully cooked. Remember to open the beverage can to avoid cooking a "thunderbird."

BURNT END'S BEER-BATTERED FRIED PICKLES WITH JALAPEÑO BBQ AIOLI

Pitmaster/chef Smoky Schwartz whips up these delicious starters on occasion, with aioli, ranch dip, and barbecue sauce dip. Serve your pickles with all three, but don't leave out the aioli. It is easy to make and worth the effort. **Makes about 50 to 75 (or more) fried pickles depending on thickness of chips**

Line cookie tray with parchment paper and dust with flour. Whisk ingredients (except for pickles) together.

Dip pickle chips into the batter and place on cookie sheet. Dust tops of pickles with flour and freeze for at least 12 hours. You can use now or portion pickle chips into individual freezer bags and return to freezer until ready to fry. Drop pickles in small batches into oil (heated to about 365°F) until golden brown, about 1 to 2 minutes. Dry on paper towels.

Serve with accompanying sauces.

Battered Fried Pickles

1½ cups flour, plus additional for dusting
1 teaspoon black pepper
½ teaspoon chili powder
¼ teaspoon cayenne pepper
½ teaspoon chipotle powder
1 (12-ounce) can beer
20 dill pickles, sliced into chips

Place all ingredients in a blender except the oil; pulse blend until smooth. Then slowly drizzle the oil into the blender running at low speed until the sauce emulsifies and thickens.

Properly label and store, refrigerated, until served as dip with beer-battered fried pickles.

Jalapeño BBQ Aioli

Makes 6 cups

1 ounce minced garlic
1 ounce minced shallot
1½ ounces minced fresh jalapeño with seeds
1½ ounces rough chopped cilantro
1½ ounces lime juice
3 egg yolks
1 ounce plain yellow mustard
1½ ounces cider vinegar
3 ounces traditional tomato base barbecue sauce (Burnt End's or your favorite brand)
¼ ounce salt
¼ ounce black pepper
2 cups vegetable oil

BROBECK'S SMOKED HAM SALAD

Grandma Brobeck is the inspiration for this recipe. Doug Brobeck learned the value of not wasting food when he was growing up in East Tennessee near Johnson City. When he started his career as a barbecue pitmaster and restaurant owner, Grandma's example was just what he needed when faced with what to do with ham and turkey scraps that were too loose for a sandwich but too good to throw away. Since he first introduced this salad to customers, he can't make enough!

This recipe is a variation of Brobecks BBQ's Original Ham Salad recipe. It is not exact, due to differences in certain ingredients Brobecks makes from scratch. It takes about 20 minutes to prepare. **Makes 10 sandwiches**

3 cups ground smoked ham
2 cups ground smoked turkey
½ cup pureed onion (or finely chopped)
¼ cup Brobecks BBQ Mustard Sauce (or spicy mustard)
1 cup mayonnaise
½ cup sweet pickle relish
⅛ teaspoon cinnamon
Pinch of cayenne pepper
¼ teaspoon black pepper
1 teaspoon Frank's Hot Sauce

In a large mixing bowl, combine all ingredients. Taste salad. If needed, season with additional black pepper or add salt to your preference.

Cover and refrigerate for several hours.

Serve as a dip with chips or crackers or spread on bread to make a sandwich. Enjoy!

EARL QUICK'S BOLO: BBQ BALONEY SANDWICH

Many Kansas City barbecue lovers, especially those with roots in Texas, Oklahoma, and Tennessee, were elated when Ron Quick, co-owner of the former Earl Quick's Bar-B-Q, added baloney to their menu. Ron said it was "sort of a novelty item" at first, but the "Bolo" sandwich gained a solid fan base. Sadly, the 50-year-old landmark restaurant on Merriam Lane closed in 2014. Quicks on Wheels, a food truck operated by Dustin Quick, sometimes offers the Bolo.

For the baloney sandwich, Quick smokes 10-pound chubs and cuts them into ¼-inch slices to deep fry prior to serving.

Since baloney is fully cooked and ready to eat, why barbecue it? Because smoke cranks it up to a whole new level of good eating. Add barbecue sauce, sides of barbecue beans and coleslaw, and a frosty beer for a memorable meal. Sometimes I top the baloney with beans and slaw for an open-face sandwich. **Makes 10–12 sandwiches**

Use a 3-pound baloney chub or a 4¼-inch-diameter chunk deli baloney. If you use smaller diameter ring baloney, cut the smoking time in half.

In a kettle cooker, put your hot coals on one side to avoid cooking the baloney directly over them.

Remove the paper encasement from the baloney. Place the baloney on an oiled grate opposite the hot coals. Sprinkle 2 cups of water-soaked/drained pecan or hickory chips on the coals. Put the lid on the kettle and let the baloney smoke slow and low, from 110°F to no higher than 125°F, for a couple of hours. Monitor the temperature with a candy thermometer in the hole in the lid. Too much heat will burst your baloney. That's not a disaster, but it makes a better presentation if it doesn't burst.

Since baloney is a finely ground, precooked sausage, you're barbecuing for flavor, not doneness.

Serve with barbecue beans and coleslaw or potato salad.

SHANNON "FIREBUG" KIMBALL'S BEEF CROSTINI WITH CARAMELIZED ONION AND FIG BALSAMIC

When you're looking for something different and flavorful from your grill, you can count on Kansas City's "Firebug" to deliver. This crostini with caramelized onion, fig balsamic, and a tender slice of grilled beef will impress your guests. **Serves 6–8**

1 loaf French bread, thinly sliced

2 tablespoons olive oil

3 red or sweet onions, thinly sliced

⅓ cup dry red wine

⅓ cup red wine vinegar

¼ cup packed light brown sugar

¼ cup honey

1 (24-ounce) piece beef tenderloin

Fig balsamic drizzle

Preheat your grill to medium-high heat.

Brush the slices of French bread with the olive oil. Grill on both sides until crispy. Set aside.

In a medium saucepan, combine the onions, wine, vinegar, brown sugar, and honey. Stir constantly over medium heat until the sugar is dissolved, about 5 minutes. Reduce heat to low and simmer for 30 minutes, until the sauce is the consistency of marmalade.

Grill the beef tenderloin, turning to mark all sides, until medium rare, 10–15 minutes total. Let rest for 10 minutes, and then thinly slice the meat. Place a slice of beef on each French bread crostini and top each with a teaspoon of onion marmalade and drizzle fig balsamic and serve.

RJ'S ORIGINAL BURNT END HASH

The Kansas City Barbeque Society's slogan, "Barbeque: it's not just for breakfast anymore," reflects our city's passion for barbecue as every meal/every day cuisine. The expression is more tongue-in-cheek than reality, however, as there are precious few barbecue joints in Kansas City that serve barbecue for breakfast. RJ's Bob-Be-Que Shack is one of the exceptions. Customers flock in every weekend for a barbecue breakfast. The Burnt End Hash is one of the most popular dishes. **Serves 4**

In large frying pan melt butter on medium heat, add mushrooms, onions, peppers and bacon. Sauté until vegetables are soft, add potatoes and burnt ends, brown lightly, and toss with dry meat rub.

Cook eggs as desired, plate individually, or serve in casserole dish.

Serve with Texas Toast and your favorite BBQ sauce.

¼ cup unsalted butter

6 ounces sliced fresh mushrooms

1 bunch sliced green onions

½ cup diced red and green peppers

6 ounces chopped crispy smoked bacon

2 cups cooked diced potatoes

24 ounces crispy beef brisket or pork burnt ends, cut in bite-size pieces

1 tablespoon R.J.'s dry meat rub

8 whole eggs, prepared any way you like, e.g., scrambled, over easy, etc.

PLOWBOYS BRISKET BURNT END POT PIE

Todd Johns told me, "I am not a chef. Never been to culinary school or worked in a kitchen until I owned my own. I am quick to correct anyone who refers to me as a chef. I haven't earned that title. Not a foodie, though I appreciate great food. I am not a baker. Couldn't make bread, cakes, or confections without a box mix and instructions. I am a cook. I cook like an old grandmother because that's who I was taught by. My dishes are comfort food, inspired by my grandma's scratch cooking. Just like her, I seldom follow a recipe but could re-create dishes if called upon. Like her, my food isn't fancy. It is filling. It is familiar to many that probably grew up on similar dishes. I owe all of my success as a cook both at home and professionally to my grandmother who taught and inspires me."

Todd continued, "This is as best as I can do to produce a recipe, since it really doesn't exist. Pot pies are something I've learned how to do in order to get rid of leftovers from BBQ contests. They are really easy and quick. This is something that could be done any night of the week for even the busiest of families."

I have eaten a slice of Todd's Brisket Burnt End Pot Pie, and can assure you that following his directions below will yield a delicious pie for your family and guests. **Serves 6–8**

1 tablespoon canola oil
1 onion, diced
Pinch of salt
3–4 cloves garlic, chopped or
    pressed (pressed is best)
⅓ cup flour
1 quart beef stock
Approximately 4 cups burnt
    ends, chopped small to
    medium size
Approximately 2 cups diced
    carrots
Approximately 2 cups fresh or
    canned green beans
⅓ cup frozen green peas
2 (9-inch) refrigerated pie
    crusts

Heat oil in a skillet. Add diced onion and sauté with the pinch of salt. Once onions are soft, add garlic and sauté for just a minute. Add flour and create a roux (grandma would just call it a gravy). Cook the roux until it turns a golden brown. This creates that earthy, nutty flavor that will bring your pot pie to life with the beef.

Add beef stock (stock is always better than broth). Here's where you may want to add a little as you go. You are looking for thick gravy as the base of your filling. Boiling creates thickness. Once the gravy is where you want it, remove from heat. It is ready.

Now add your chopped burnt ends. The recipe calls for about 4 cups, but to be honest, I don't measure. I add as much as I want to add.

Blanch the diced carrots until al dente (cooked but firm) and add them to the burnt end and gravy mixture. Again, use as much as you want, a couple cups. Add the green beans If they are fresh, blanch them first.

Finally, add frozen peas. Peas are tender, and you don't want to destroy them by overcooking. Frozen peas will thaw quickly in the hot gravy.

Press one crust into a pie plate. Pre-greasing the pan is not required. Add your filling to the top and place the top crust. Pinch the two crusts to close and brush the top with egg wash.

Bake at 375°F until crust is golden brown, 15–20 minutes.

DAN JANSSEN'S SMOKED MEATLOAF

Meatloaf is America's favorite way to stretch meat servings. Added flavor options such as chopped peppers or onions are infinite. We make it with what's on hand or we follow a favorite tried and true recipe, especially an old family recipe that reminds us of a treasured relative. Try this outstanding combo of classic meatloaf ingredients with a barbecue lover's Kansas City–style accent. Serve with fresh, local, seasonal sides for perfect balance. **Serves 6–8**

In a mixing bowl thoroughly mix ground beef, barbecue sauce, eggs, mustard, fresh bread crumbs, and seasonings. Divide meat into 2 pieces and form your meat loaves. Make sure they are tight and firm like a football. This will ensure the product doesn't fall apart during smoking.

In a medium-hot sauté pan add oil and onions. Cook (or "sweat") onions on medium heat for 8–12 minutes until they began to turn brown and caramelized. Add barbecue sauce.

Preheat smoker using your favorite wood to 250°F. Place meatloaves on the smoker grates and top each with caramelized onions. Smoke until internal temperature reaches 160°F. Use a large barbecue spatula to remove the meatloaves from smoker and let them rest for 10 minutes. Slice and serve.

Meatloaf

Makes 2 (1½-pound) loaves

2½ pounds ground beef

¼ cup barbecue sauce

2 eggs

⅛ cup mustard

1–2 cups fresh bread crumbs

2 tablespoons rub

2 teaspoons salt

1 teaspoon pepper

Caramelized Onions

1 tablespoon olive oil

1 medium onion sliced

½ cup barbecue sauce

RABBI MENDEL SEGAL'S BBQ BEEF KNISH

Barbecue is a citywide passion in Kansas City. Although we love our traditional Southern sides and entrees, we don't let tradition get in the way of new ways to enjoy our barbecue. Try Rabbi Segal's Kansas City–style barbecue beef knish and you'll shout a "Geshmak" of approval! **Makes 6–12 knishes, depending on size**

2 cups flour
2 teaspoons baking powder
1 teaspoon salt
¼ cup margarine
¾ cup apple juice, divided
Barbecue brisket
Barbecue sauce
1 egg, beaten, for glaze

Preheat oven to 350°F.

In a large bowl sift flour, baking soda, and salt. Cut margarine in until dough is the consistency of course crumbs. Add ½ cup apple juice and mix. Add the rest of the apple juice a bit at a time until dough can be gathered in a ball. Knead for 1 minute, cover and refrigerate for 30 minutes. (If you're in a time crunch Pillsbury pastry dough works, too.)

Roll dough thin, and using a cup or a bowl, cut dough into circles. Fill center of dough with barbecue brisket tossed in barbecue sauce. Bring the sides up, pinch together tightly, and flip over. Coat with egg wash.

Bake 20–35 minutes until golden brown.

B.B.'S LAWNSIDE MEMPHIS MINNIE'S SMOKED CATFISH

This entree at B.B.'s was inspired by travels to blues festivals in Louisiana and blues adventures in the Mississippi Delta by BB's co-owners, Lindsay & Jo Shannon. There they enjoyed an abundance of smoked catfish. Since B.B.'s already has the blues, why not add smoked catfish! It is named after blues legend Lizzie Douglas, who started her career as a runaway at age 13, singing on Beale Street sidewalks in Memphis. She made an indelible footprint on the blues.

B.B.'s Lawnside Memphis Minnie's Smoked Catfish is so good that it was featured by Anthony Bourdain on his show *No Reservations*. When I asked Lindsay for the recipe, he replied, "The first order of business to smoke catfish is to find a granite stone pit that was built in 1950. The rest is easy."

Easier yet is to go to B.B.'s, where pitmaster Mike Nickle will smoke a delicious catfish for you in B.B.'s granite stone pit. Lindsay and Mike gave me these tips for a homestyle version. **Serves 1–2**

Sprinkle all surfaces of the fish with lemon pepper. Smoke at 190–225°F for 2½–3 hours, until meat is tender and flaky. Serve immediately.

At the restaurant, Lindsay and Jo recommend their homestyle coleslaw and battered fries on the side, as featured in Guy Fieri's show *Diners, Drive-Ins and Dives*.

Lindsay also shared a recommended playlist for listening as you cook and eat the fish:

Taj Mahal, "Catfish Blues"

Muddy Waters, "Rollin' Stone"

Robert Petway, "Catfish Blues" (1941)

Tommy McClennan, "Deep Blue Sea Blues"

Jim Jackson, "Kansas City Blues"

1 whole (15- to 17-ounce) catfish per serving (They use farm-raised catfish, cleaned, head removed, bone in, skin on.)

3 tablespoons lemon pepper per fish

SQUEAL LIKE A PIG BUTTERMILK HUSH PUPPIES

Kansas City visitors from the South, especially North Carolina, will be surprised and disappointed when a basket of hush puppies isn't at hand to munch on as they study the menu in a local barbecue joint—or if hush puppies don't automatically arrive with their order. Slap's is one of the few places in town that visitors hungry for hush puppies can count on. These puppies are a big hit with local Kansas City barbecue lovers and visitors! These fantastic traditional puppies are ready to serve in only 35 minutes total. Thanks to Joe Pearce for the recipe.   **Makes 8**

6 cups vegetable oil
1½ cups self-rising white
   cornmeal mix
¾ cup self-rising flour
¾ cup diced sweet onion
   (about ½ medium onion)
1½ tablespoons sugar
1 large egg, lightly beaten
1¼ cups buttermilk

Pour oil to depth of 3 inches in a 4-quart Dutch oven; heat to 375°F.

Combine cornmeal and next 3 ingredients. Add egg and buttermilk; stir just until moistened. Let stand 10 minutes.

Drop batter by rounded tablespoonful into hot oil, and fry, in 3 batches, 2–3 minutes on each side or until golden. Keep warm in a 200°F oven.

AUGUSTA'S SAVORY CRUNCHY SLAW BY SMOKE 'N' FIRE

Jim Cattey, co-owner of Smoke 'n' Fire with his wife, Joan, developed this recipe in honor of his mother, Augusta Sheen Cattey of Brookfield, Missouri. She lived a full and generous life of 90 years. In addition to running Cattey Feed & Seed in Brookfield for many years with Jim's dad, Nelson Cattey, Augusta was active in her church, 4-H, and the American Angus Association. Augusta loved to garden and to gather relatives and friends around her table to enjoy the bounties of her garden. There is good slaw, and there is fantastic slaw. This one is fantastic! **Serves 4**

Remove the tough outer leaves of the cabbage head and cut the head in half from top of core. Remove the core and set aside for snacking with seasoned pepper. Slice the cabbage halves very thinly with a sharp slicer knife. Put the cabbage shreds in a glass serving bowl, cover the bowl with plastic wrap, and chill the cabbage, keeping it separate until serving time.

In a non-reactive sauce pan, use a whisk or stick blender to combine the oil and vinegar with all other ingredients except salt. Bring the blend to a simmer until the sugar is dissolved. Pour into a dressing boat and allow the blend to sit and cool for at least an hour for the flavors to combine. This creates the dressing.

Just before serving toss the cabbage and the dressing together and dust with the sea salt for fresh crispy slaw.

La Tourangelle Grapeseed Oil & Smoke 'n' Fire Seasoned Pepper is available for purchase at Smoke 'n' Fire online or in person.

1 medium head of cabbage, thinly sliced, 1/16–1/8 inch

1/8 cup grapeseed oil, La Tourangelle or your favorite brand

1/4 cup white vinegar

1 clove garlic, squeezed through fine mesh garlic press

1 teaspoon sugar

1–2 teaspoons seasoned pepper (to taste), Smoke 'n' Fire or your favorite brand

1/2 teaspoon sea salt, reserved until serving

KANSAS CITY STYLE BARBECUE BEANS

Kansas City barbecue lovers have a great appreciation for the pinto beans served in Texas barbecue joints. In Kansas City, however, we expect a different style of bean. We want barbecue meat with our beans. We also want them laced with barbecue sauce. And we're okay with pinto, great northern, or combos of three or four different kinds of beans. Meat and sauce distinguish Kansas City–style beans from others. Variations on the theme are endless. Here's a basic favorite, adapted from what I learned years ago from Chef Paul Kirk, KC Baron of Barbecue. **Serves 8**

2 strips thick bacon

1 medium-size sweet Texas or Vidalia onion, chopped

1 red bell pepper, chopped

5 (15-ounce) cans pork and beans, drained and rinsed

1 (4-ounce) can diced mild chile peppers

2 cups chopped barbecued brisket, burnt ends, or rib pieces

2 cups Kansas City tomato base barbecue sauce; I always use at least one cup of the hometown favorite, KC Masterpiece

⅓ cup prepared mustard

1 tablespoon brown sugar

Water or beer, for thinning

Fry the bacon and set it aside. Sauté the onion and bell pepper in the bacon grease until tender. Crumble the bacon.

Rinse the beans in a screened colander. They will retain some flavor, but if not drained, your beans will taste like doctored-up pork and beans, not Kansas City–style barbecue beans.

Put the beans, crumbled bacon, onion, bell peppers, chile peppers, barbecue meat, barbecue sauce, mustard, and brown sugar in a ceramic casserole. Thin with water or beer, as needed.

Bake the beans in an oven or barbecue grill—opposite direct heat—uncovered, for 3 hours at 225°F. Stir occasionally during cooking.

Experiment with your own variations of this basic recipe. Your friends will say you make the best barbecue beans they've ever tasted.

JON RUSSELL'S WHITE BEAN & CHICKEN CHILI – HOMESTYLE

Jon Niederbremer and Russell Muehlberger have competed at the Great Lenexa Barbeque Battle and other barbecue contests for more than two decades, winning a fair share of ribbons, trophies, and cash. They are also longtime competitors at the annual Lenexa Chili Challenge, sanctioned by the Chili Appreciation Society International (CASI). They won First Place in the Homestyle category in 2013. Since CASI rules forbid the use of beans, pasta, rice, hominy, corn, or similar "fillers," this White Bean & Chicken Chili would be disqualified in a CASI-sanctioned contest. It's a winner at the restaurant, however, and this homestyle version will win favor with your family and friends. Thanks to Tracy Mandel McHugh, President of 39th Street Bevco of Kansas LLC, owner of Jon Russell's Kansas City Barbeque, for her guidance with this homestyle adaptation. When you can't make it to the restaurant, try this.

Serves 6–8

Sauté the peppers and onion with olive oil in a 3-quart stainless steel soup pot. Add other ingredients and simmer, uncovered, for 20–30 minutes.

- 1 tablespoon extra-virgin olive oil
- 1 fire-roasted mild or hot (your choice) Poblano pepper, seeded and chopped, or 1 (4-ounce) can diced green chiles
- 1 medium-size white or sweet onion, diced
- 1 garlic clove, minced
- ½ green fire-roasted bell pepper, diced
- 1½ pounds roasted boneless/skinless chicken breast, minced

- 1 (10-ounce) can Ro*Tel Original Mild diced tomatoes & green chilies
- 3 (15.5-ounce) cans cannellini beans, drained and rinsed.
- 1½ quarts chicken stock
- 2 cups fire-roasted corn kernels (frozen or canned will work)
- ½ tablespoon powdered cumin
- ½ teaspoon powdered oregano
- Salt and pepper to taste
- 2 bay leaves

DALTON GANG CHILI

Any imagined connection between the infamous bank-robbing Dalton Gang that once called Coffeyville, Kansas, their hometown is unfounded. This chili is named after a famous Kansas City barbecue personality, Pat Dalton, one of the founders of the Great Lenexa BBQ Battle. Instead of robbing banks, Pat Dalton's family has been in the florist business since 1941. Pat himself served as principal of St. Agnes Elementary School in Fairway, Kansas, for many years.

What's special about this recipe is its important role in the 2nd Annual Diddy-Wa-Diddy National Barbecue Sauce Contest. The year was 1985. The contest was a fundraiser to save 300 acres of Olathe prairie, woodlands, and wetlands from housing and business development. KC Baron of Barbecue Chef Paul Kirk, KC Rib Doctor Guy Simpson, and Pat Dalton of the Dalton Gang Competition Barbecue Team, served as official pitmasters. They endured a cold, rainy, lonely prairie night, serenaded by howling coyotes. Pat sustained them with Dalton Gang Chili. To this day it is the greatest chili I've ever tasted, bar none.

By midmorning the next day, the Baron/Rib Doctor/Dalton Gang team was ready to serve hungry crowds hundreds of pounds of barbecue beef brisket, pork butt, ribs, and chicken. Today the Prairie Center is owned and managed by the Kansas Department of Wildlife, Parks and Tourism. It is enjoyed by thousands of metro Kansas City urbanites. Never underestimate the power of barbecue and a pot of Dalton Gang Chili. Thanks to Pat for sharing this recipe. **Serves 6–8**

1 pound ground beef
1 pound ground pork
1 medium to large onion,
   diced
2 (15-ounce) cans pinto beans
2 (15-ounce) cans black beans
2 (8-ounce) cans tomato sauce
1 (15-ounce) can diced
   tomatoes
Cumin to taste
Chili powder to taste
Ground ancho chiles to taste
Salt to taste

Combine meat and onion. Brown and drain. Add beans, tomato sauce, and diced tomatoes. Season with cumin, chili powder, ground ancho chiles, and salt to taste. Simmer until all ingredients mix well together.

RICKY'S PIT BBQ CHILI

Ricky Smith is known throughout Kansas City for his barbecue and chili. Both are so good that you needn't toss a coin to decide which one you're going to enjoy on any given day. Have both. If you're lucky, Ricky will give you a sample taste of chili to seal the deal before you order.

Many have begged Ricky for his recipe, but he hasn't parted with it—until now. I guess he was feeling especially generous when I asked. Here it is, straight from Ricky:

> "A lot of that,
> Some of this,
> And a little bit of that."

This recipe serves as many as you wish, and there's no clean-up!

SUMMIT HICKORY PIT BBQ CHEESY POTATO CASSEROLE

Thanks to Katy Birchfield, Summit Hickory Pit BBQ owner, for this exclusive and very popular Cheesy Potato Casserole recipe. This is a scaled-down version. **Serves 4–6**

Stir all ingredients together until creamy. Pour into casserole dish. Bake at 350°F for 35–40 minutes.

4–6 potatoes, cooked, peeled, and coarsely chopped
1 tablespoon garlic powder
1 tablespoon seasoned salt
1 teaspoon ground black pepper
2 sprigs fresh parsley, chopped
1 cup shredded cheddar cheese
1 cup sour cream
1 cup milk

HAWGFATHERS HOT POTATO SALAD

Jay "The Snail" Vantuyl is one of the most inventive pitmaster talents in Kansas City. He knows the contest scene. He knows the cuisine scene, from pits to plates. Jay is one of my go-to friends for information about barbecue or darned near any other topic. His curiosity about humankind and our planet knows no bounds. He has extended his professional sign painting talents to watercolor still lifes from nature, plus animated mythical characters such as the "Mugwump" and a half frog/half chicken known as a "Fricken."

When Jay tells me, "I know a barbecue place that if you haven't tried it, I think you'll be glad to know about it," I listen. More often than not, he'll meet me there to compare tasting notes.

That's what happened when Jay told me about A Little BBQ Joint in Independence. Besides the fantastic barbecue there, one of our favorite sides is the hot potato salad. Here's the result when I asked him if he could come up with a homestyle version.

A Little BBQ Joint also offers hot potato salad as a Potato Boat entree, topped with barbecue pulled pork. **Serves 4–6**

1 (32-ounce) package frozen diced hash brown potatoes
1 tablespoon canola or peanut oil as required for potatoes
5 slices hickory-smoked bacon
¼ cup distilled white vinegar
2 tablespoons water
⅓ cup dehydrated chopped onions
1 tablespoon dehydrated green peppers
½ teaspoon salt
½ teaspoon sugar
½ teaspoon pepper
⅔ cup cream cheese
⅓ cup ranch dressing
⅔ cup whole milk
1 (15-ounce) carton sour cream
1 cup shredded cheddar cheese

Prepare frozen hash browns as instructed on package.

Cut bacon in 1-inch pieces and fry in a separate skillet until crisp.

Add vinegar, water, dehydrated onions and peppers, along with the three spices, to bacon in skillet. Heat until onions and peppers are reconstituted. Add in the hot prepared hash browns. Warm all ingredients and mix well with cream cheese, ranch dressing, milk, sour cream, and shredded cheddar. Serve warm.

Other options: Season with your choice of the following ingredients: garlic salt or garlic pepper, celery salt, fresh or dried chives or parsley.

Can be prepared with fresh ingredients instead of dehydrated.

BIG 'UNS HEART ATTACK FRIES

The name gives you fair warning. This heavenly dish is loaded with the good stuff! Channel your inner Pythagoras and enjoy now and then in moderation. Heaven can wait. **Serves 1–2**

Top the hot fries with cheese first, then meat. Serve immediately with your choice of condiment on the side.

- 6 ounces fries
- 6 ounces shredded cheddar cheese
- ¼ cup bacon bits
- 8 ounces warm pulled pork, chopped brisket, sliced sausage, turkey slices, or sliced hot links
- 2 ounces barbecue sauce, sour cream, or ranch dressing on the side

CHAR BAR JO-JO POTATOES

Seasoned fried potatoes have come to be known as "Jo-Jo's." My favorites until I ate at Kansas City's Char Bar were served by pitmaster/owner Moses Quartey at Ted's 19th Hole in Minneapolis. Although Ted's Jo-Jo's are still on my favorites list, Executive Chef Jeremy Tawney's Char Bar rendition of Jo-Jo's is my new fav. The unique seasonings put Jeremy's Jo-Jo's over-the-top in flavor. They go well with any barbecue meat, Kansas City style or elsewhere. **Serves 4–6**

Mix the dry ingredients; store, covered, until ready for use.

Bake potatoes in a 400°F oven for 45 minutes. Set aside to cool; refrigerate, covered, for 1 hour or overnight until ready for use.

To prepare, cut each potato into quarters, skin on. In a cast iron skillet, pan-fry the potatoes in vegetable oil until crisp and golden.

Stir together the seasoning and potatoes in a mixing bowl and toss with a wooden spoon to evenly coat.

Serve immediately.

- 2 cups powdered cheese
- 1 cup barbecue rub, your favorite (Chef Tawney uses Char Bar's signature Meat Mitch rub)
- 5 large russet potatoes, scrubbed clean, skin on
- 1 cup malt vinegar
- ¼ cup vegetable oil

ARTHUR BRYANT'S–STYLE FRIES

Barbecue at Arthur Bryant's without the famous fries is unthinkable to Kansas City barbecue lovers. I asked former longtime co-owner Gary Berbiglia for some tips on cooking Arthur Bryant's–style fries. He told me they always sought Idaho russet potatoes, "as large and lengthy as possible." Furthermore, "We never used salt in any part of the process, before blanching or after cooking." Your best bet is to enjoy the fries on location at Arthur Bryant's. When you crave them, and going there is not an option, here's how to make Bryant's-style fries at home. Taste the finished fries sans salt. Add salt to your taste if you must. Be extra attentive to safety precautions when cooking with hot lard. **Serves 4**

4 pounds pure lard

4 large Idaho russet potatoes, washed, unpeeled, cut into about 5/16-inch french fry-style pieces

Heat the lard to 325°F in a deep fryer.

Divide fries into 8 batches and blanch each batch for about 3 minutes in the hot lard. Drain each batch on paper towels or on a wire rack. Put the blanched fries in a cooler and let cool, covered, for at least 30 minutes.

Five minutes before you're ready to serve the fries, drop them in hot lard in batches and fry them for 4–5 minutes until golden crisp on the outside. Enjoy the sweet, crispy outside/soft inside fries that helped make Arthur Bryant's famous. Never salted.

JACK STACK CHEESY CORN BAKE

Cheesy Corn Bake is a Jack Stack classic loved by all. This homestyle version will work for you when you can't dine in one of the Jack Stack restaurants. **Serves 10–12**

In a 4-quart sauce pan, melt butter over low heat. Stir in the flour and garlic powder until well blended, then add milk all at once.

Cook over medium heat, stirring constantly to prevent scorching, until thickened and bubbly.

Stir in cream cheese and cheddar cheese sauce, and continue cooking until cheese is melted.

Stir in corn and ham.

Transfer mixture to a 2-quart casserole dish. Bake at 350°F for 45 minutes.

Note: Although the recipe used in the Jack Stack restaurants and shipped product is gluten-free, this home-version contains flour and is therefore NOT gluten-free.

2 tablespoons butter

4 teaspoons all-purpose flour

⅛ teaspoon garlic powder

¾ cup milk

1 (3-ounce) package cream cheese, cut into 1-inch cubes

6 ounces sharp cheddar cheese

3 (10-ounce) packages frozen whole kernel corn, thawed

3 ounces smoked ham, diced

Adult Beverages that Pair Well with Barbecue

Water, iced tea, and soda are standard beverage offerings at Kansas City barbecue joints. Many offer major national brand beers such as Budweiser, Miller, or Coors. Increasing numbers of establishments are offering craft beers from the metro area and beyond. Some, like Q39 and Char Bar, offer enough variety that a licensed cicerone could easily carve a niche there. Likewise, expanded wine menus in some joints could make room for an in-house sommelier.

Beer Pairings

Sarah Hearn at Cinder Block Brewery suggested these beer pairings with barbecue:

Pavers Porter (hearty bold dark beer with hints of chocolate): Burnt ends, brisket, or anything that has been smoked

Weathered Wit (Belgian-style wheat beer with notes of coriander and orange): Any chicken dish

Prime EPA (balance of malt and hoppiness in medium-bodied beer): Ribs and any barbecue with a little kick

Block IPA (light-bodied IPA full of flavorful hoppy goodness): Spicy barbecue would be great with the hops

Northtown Native (California Common–style beer that is light and easy drinking, the beer for the new craft beer drinker): Goes well with any barbecue

Craft beers to look for in select Kansas City barbecue restaurants

Boulevard Wheat

Boulevard Pale Ale

Cinder Block IPA

Cinder Block North Town Native

Cinder Block Pavers Porter

Cinder Block Prime Extra Pale Ale

Cinder Block Weathered Wit

Flying Monkey Amber Ale

Flying Monkey Four-Finger Stout

Flying Monkey Mac's Beer

Flying Monkey Wheat Beer

Free State

Free State

Tallgrass Buffalo Sweat

Tallgrass Velvet Rooster

New beers appear frequently in the rapidly growing craft beer industry. Ask your server for tips on current favorites in their restaurant.

Wine Pairings

Some say dry red wines pair best with beef and lamb; white, dry or sweet, with poultry and pork. Others say Zinfandel pairs well with any barbecue meat. It's completely a matter of personal taste. Like Stan Nelson told me, "The best wine with barbecue is the wine you like with barbecue." Enough said.

Whiskey

I'm a before and/or after man. Whiskey with barbecue doesn't dance on my palate, but a shot before or after a barbecue meal—that's my dance! On special occasions I like to toast the pitmaster and present company with a sip of quality whiskey, neat or on the rocks. When Jack Daniel's is in the glass, fond memories of friends past and present are evoked—especially over the past 25 years and counting at the Jack Daniel's World Championship Invitational Barbecue, aka The Jack.

Three Kansas City favorites are:

Dark Horse Distillery

11740 W 86th Ter., Lenexa, KS 66214; (913) 492-3275; www.dhdistillery.com
Master distiller: Patrick Garcia

Their current line of spirits is Reunion Rye, Reserve Bourbon, Long Shot White Whiskey, and Rider Vodka.

They sell charred (medium #3 char) American oak mini wooden barrels in three sizes—2-liter, 5-liter, 10-liter—for extra aging of your whiskey, or for mixing cocktails, sauces, or other beverages of your choosing. Can be cleaned and reused numerous times.

High Plains Distillery

1700 Rooks Rd., Atchison, KS 66002 (about 17 miles northwest of the US Penitentiary, Leavenworth, and 24 miles from the Kansas State Penitentiary, Lansing); (913) 773-5780; http://highplainsinc.com
Seth & Dorcie Fox; daughter Sierra and son Hunter
Vodka, flavored vodkas, gin and Pioneer Whiskey

J. Rieger & Company

2700 Guinotte Ave., Kansas City, MO 64120; http://jriegerco.com
Almost 100 years ago, J. Rieger's distillery was in the historic West Bottoms. Recently revived in the East Bottoms by co-founders Ryan Maybee and Andy Rieger, it has become an instant Kansas City favorite. What's not to like about a distilled blend of corn, malt, and rye with a touch of sherry? Best to sip this 92 proof masterpiece like moonshine, slow and easy, as a perfect ending to a barbecue feast. Go online for J. Rieger's Horsefeather and Old Fashioned recipes.

DANNY EDWARDS APPLE PIE CRUMBLE TOP

Danny Edwards, one of Kansas City's favorite pitmasters, is multitalented. Try this pie and you'll agree that Danny should add "pie-master" to his culinary credentials. **Makes 1 pie**

Filling

6 cups Granny Smith apples, peeled and sliced ¼-inch thick
1 cup brown sugar
¼ cup flour
2 tablespoons butter, cut in dots
1 teaspoon cinnamon
½ teaspoon fresh nutmeg
Pinch of salt
1 (9-inch) pie shell

Put all ingredients except pie shell in a glass bowl for 15 minutes, until juicy. Pour into pie shell.

Crumble Topping

½ cup oatmeal
½ cup chopped pecans or walnuts
½ cup flour
½ cup brown sugar
½ teaspoon cinnamon
4 tablespoon butter

Combine all ingredients except butter. Cut butter into mixture with fingers.

Top pie with crumbles. Bake 55 minutes at 350°F until golden brown on top.

Let set before slicing.

DANNY EDWARDS BREAD PUDDING

Not every barbecue joint in Kansas City pays homage to this classic barbecue joint dessert. Danny makes one of the best! **Serves 12**

In a large mixing bowl combine the eggs, brown sugar, cinnamon, nutmeg, and vanilla, and whisk to blend. Whisk in the heavy cream and milk.

In a separate bowl, mix bread heels with nuts and Craisins.

Fold into egg mixture. Cover with plastic wrap and refrigerate for 2 hours.

Preheat oven to 350°F. Grease 12 muffin tins with butter.

Spoon the mixture evenly into the muffin tins, then place the tins on a baking sheet. Bake until the centers spring back when touched, 20–35 minutes. Remove from the oven and let cool for about 5 minutes.

Serve warm.

5 eggs

1 cup brown sugar

2 teaspoons cinnamon

1 teaspoon nutmeg

2 teaspoons vanilla

4 cups heavy cream

1 cup milk

8 cups bread heels (cut into small pieces)

1 cup chopped walnuts or pecans

1 cup Craisins

SHANNON "FIREBUG" KIMBALL'S GRILLED PEACHES WITH PORT WINE SAUCE

Creativity reigns when the "Firebug" is at the grill. Peaches take on a refreshing explosion of flavors in this dish. You and your guests will love it. **Serves 10–12**

Combine peaches, wine, brown sugar, bay leaves, pepper, and salt in an airtight container and let marinate for 4–6 hours.

Remove peaches and pour marinade into a saucepan. Reduce by 75 percent over medium heat.

Remove from heat, strain, and stir in butter just before serving.

Meanwhile, grill peaches over live fire (fruitwood is best) until caramelized. Serve with a scoop of vanilla ice cream and port wine sauce drizzled over the top. Take it to the next level and sprinkle a pinch of Fruitwood Smoked Sea Salt over this dessert!

6–8 fresh firm peaches, cut in half with seed removed

1 quart port wine or sweet red wine

⅛ cup brown sugar

2 bay leaves

1 teaspoon fresh ground black pepper

1 teaspoon kosher salt

3 tablespoons unsalted butter

Vanilla ice cream for serving

Q39 APPLE CRUMBLE

I have no argument with those who say barbecue is as American as apple pie. Why not have both? Although I usually fill up on barbecue, there are a few desserts that are so good that no matter how full you are, you'll be glad you tried it. Rob Magee's Q39 Apple Crumble is one of those desserts. **Serves 4–6**

Fruit

2 pounds Granny Smith apples, peeled, cored, and sliced ¼-inch thick

1 tablespoon freshly squeezed lemon juice

⅓ cup flour

2 tablespoons sugar

¼ teaspoon cinnamon

Crumble

½ cup brown sugar

¼ cup flour

¾ cup quick oats

2 teaspoons cinnamon

Pinch of salt

¾ stick butter, cubed and cold

Toss apples, lemon juice, flour, sugar, and cinnamon.

Spray baking dishes with nonstick spray and fill with coated apples. Be sure to mound over the top of the dishes—apples will lose volume and sink down after baking.

In a mixing bowl, combine brown sugar, flour, oats, cinnamon, and salt. Mix on low speed until evenly combined.

Add butter all at once, keeping mixer on low, until pea-size bits of butter remain. It is important that butter is cold, or else it will cream into crumble mixture and won't bake properly. Crumb topping should be sandy and crumbly.

Heap crumble over apple slices until covered; press down gently to keep it in place.

Bake at 350°F for 30 minutes, until apples are just done. Leave at room temperature until ready to serve. Before serving, place crumble in 350°F oven to warm for 5–7 minutes. Spoon onto plate and serve with scoop of vanilla ice cream in center.

CHAR BAR VELVET ELVIS

Memphis has Leonard's Pit Barbecue and other favorite Elvis barbecue hangouts. There's also Memphis's legendary Sun Studio, Graceland, Beale Street, the Memphis in May World Championship Barbecue Contest, and my favorite barbecue spaghetti at the Bar-B-Q Shop. Kansas City loves Memphis, and we love Elvis. So-called "high class" critics may snicker at screenprint art on velvet cloth and Graceland's Jungle Room, but they will bark like a hound dog in heat when Chef Jeremy Tawney's Velvet Elvis meets their palates.

Velvet Elvis is an inventive combination of sliced banana bread, layered and frozen peanut butter ice cream, banana rum sauce, whipped cream, coffee infused hot fudge, Cracker Jacks, spiced walnuts, and bourbon-soaked cherry.

Here's how to make it at home. When you're in Kansas City, save yourself the trouble and let Jeremy do the honors. **Serves 8**

Combine oil, sugar, and eggs in a large mixer and beat hard with a whisk until the color is light and creamy. Add bananas and vanilla extract to the mixer and combine. Add flour and baking soda and mix until the batter is creamy. Remove bowl from mixer. Fold in the chopped walnuts until evenly combined with batter.

Pour batter into greased loaf pan. Bake at 350°F for 50 minutes. Test with toothpick; should come out clean.

Cool on cooling rack. Wrap and place in freezer.

Combine ingredients in a large mixer and blend.

Combine egg white with sugar and spices. Toss nuts with egg mixture to coat evenly. Place coated nuts on a sheet pan with non-stick spray. Bake in oven at 350°F for 5 minutes. Remove and cool. Once cooled, store in an airtight container.

Banana Bread

Makes 1 loaf

1 cups vegetable oil

2 cups sugar

4 eggs

2 bananas

½ tablespoon vanilla extract

2½ cups flour

½ tablespoon baking soda

¾ cup walnuts, chopped

Peanut Butter Ice Cream

Makes 1 quart

½ pound peanut butter (Jif brand preferred)

¾ gallon vanilla bean ice cream

Spiced Nuts

Makes 1 cup

⅔ –1 egg white, whipped into soft peaks

½ tablespoon sugar

1 teaspoon cinnamon

Pinch of cayenne pepper

Pinch of nutmeg

½ pound walnuts or pecans

Cracker Jacks

2 (1-ounce) boxes

Banana Rum Sauce

Makes 1 cup

1 ounce butter
¾ tablespoon dark rum
2 tablespoons brown sugar
Pinch of cinnamon
½ banana, sliced into ¼-inch
   rounds
¼ banana, sliced into ¼-inch
   rounds and frozen

Melt butter, rum, and brown sugar in a small sauce pot, stirring often, until it is a smooth caramel. Add cinnamon and sliced room temperature bananas and continue cooking until bananas start to break down. Remove from heat and add frozen banana slices.

Coffee-Infused Hot Fudge

Makes ½ gallon

1 cup roasted coffee beans
½ gallon hot fudge

Steep coffee beans in hot fudge.

Whiskey-Soaked Cherries

Makes 10 ounces

1 (10-ounce) jar maraschino
   cherries
Jack Daniel's Tennessee Fire

Although Elvis was born in Tupelo, Mississippi, his career and fame started and ended in Memphis, Tennessee, better than 4 hours away by car from the Jack Daniel's Distillery in Lynchburg. Therefore I prefer to soak my Velvet Elvis cherries in Jack Daniels Tennessee Fire instead of Kentucky bourbon.

Drain syrup from a 10-ounce jar of maraschino cherries, leaving the cherries in the jar. Fill the jar of cherries with Jack Daniel's Tennessee Fire. Tighten the lid and store the cherries at room temperature. After one week, use cherries individually as needed.

Assemble Velvet Elvis in 8 individual ceramic cereal bowls. Place a large scoop of peanut butter ice cream between two slices of banana bread in each bowl. Garnish with spiced nuts and ¼ ounce Cracker Jacks per serving. Pour about 2 tablespoons banana rum sauce over each serving Add whipped cream and top with a whiskey-soaked cherry. Serve immediately.

Kansas City Barbecue Resources

The best way to learn the art and science of Kansas City barbecue is hands-on, with a mentor who can spare you many trial and error stumbles. It is also important to turn to books, articles, websites, blogs, archives, conferences, and videos. Remember to mingle with barbecue fans at barbecue joints, barbecue contests, and any gathering where meat fires are burning and you are invited.

Books

These books about Kansas City barbecue are good to read before or during your adventures. Most of the books listed below are out-of-print, but used copies are available online.

All About Bar-B-Q, Kansas City Style, Rich Davis and Shifra Stein (Kansas City, MO: Barbacoa Press, 1985).

All About Bar-B-Q: Kansas City-Style, 2nd edition, Rich Davis and Shifra Stein (Kansas City, MO: Pig Out Publications, 1997).

The All-American Barbecue Book: The Experts' Guide to Authentic Barbecuing, Kansas City to the Carolinas, Memphis to the Lone Star State, Rich Davis and Shifra Stein (NY: Vintage Books, 1988).

Barbecue—A Global History, Jonathan Deutsch and Megan J. Elias (London, UK: Reaktion Book, 2014)
This British co-author team's comprehensive scholarly history of barbecue in a thin 142-page tome covers an amazing amount of detail with a broad global scope. They leave no meat fire cold embers unexamined. History, differences in methods, plus old recipes, illustrations, and photos, are presented with scholarly competence sans snobbery. There will never be a book that prints the last word on barbecue. This one sets a high standard.

The Grand Barbecue: A Celebration of the History, Personalities and Techniques of Kansas City Barbecue, Doug Worgul (Kansas City, MO: Kansas City Star Books, 2001).

Kansas City BBQ Pocket Guide, Remus Powers, Ph.B. (Kansas City, MO: Pig Out Publications, 1992).

The Passion of Barbeque: The Kansas City Barbeque Society Cookbook (Kansas City, MO: Westport Publishers Inc., 1988). The first ever KCBS recipe book, assembled by Bruce Daniel, when KCBS had a total membership of 258; today's total exceeds 20,000.

Real Barbecue: The Classic Barbecue Guide to the Best Joints Across the USA—with Recipes, Porklore, and More!, Vince Staten & Greg Johnson (Guilford, CT: The Globe Pequot Press, 2007).

Real Barbecue: A Guide to the Best Joints, the Best Sauces, the Best Cookers—& Much More, Greg Johnson & Vince Staten (NY: Harper & Row, 1988).

Additional Resource for Books

Pig Out Publications
World's largest selection of barbecue-related books
6005 Martway, Suite 107
Mission, KS 66202
(913) 789-9594
www.pigoutpublications.com

Buying Meat

Kansas City's supermarkets and grocery stores offer prepackaged meats and onsite meat cutters available to answer questions and handle special requests. They also carry a variety of local and national brand barbecue sauces and rubs. Savvy barbecue cooks get acquainted with the meat staff in their neighborhood market.

Anton's Meats – Taproom/Restaurant

1610 Main St.
Kansas City, MO 64108
(816) 888-8800
http://antonskc.com
Charcuterie, steaks, grilled items, meat selection; whipped bone marrow and butter sauce; meat to go: beef, poultry, pork, steak.

Bichelmeyer Meats

704 Cheyenne Ave.
Kansas City, KS 66105
(913) 342-5945
http://bichelmeyermeatskc.com

Longtime purveyor of quality meats since 1946 and a favorite source of barbecue contest meats for many teams. Remember to get a bottle or more of Dad's Come Back Sauce.

Broadway Butcher Shop

3828 Broadway – Westport
Kansas City, MO 64111
(816) 931-2333

Dodge City Beef LLC

11101 Johnson Dr.
Shawnee, KS 66203
(913) 647-8796
www.dodgecitybeef.com
Neighborhood retail purveyor of high quality, all-natural, hormone and antibiotic-free beef, pork, bison, and lamb, along with a variety of barbecue sauces, seasonings, and rubs.

Local Pig

2618 Guinotte Ave.
Kansas City, MO 64120
(816) 200-1639
www.thelocalpig.com

McGonigle's Market

1307 W 79th St.
Kansas City, MO 64114
(816) 444-4720
https://www.mcgonigles.com

Paradise Locker Meats

405 W Birch St,
Trimble, MO 64492
(816) 370-6328
www.paradisemeats.com

Werner's Fine Sausages

5736 Johnson Dr.
Mission, KS 66202
(913) 362-5955
http://wernerswurst.com

Supermarkets

Aldi
Brookside Market
Cosentino's
Costco
Hen House
Hy-Vee
Natural Grocers
Price Chopper
Save-A-Lot

Sprouts
Sunfresh
Target
Thriftway
Trader Joe's
Wal-Mart
Wal-Mart Neighborhood Market
Wegmans
Whole Foods

Sauces, Dry Seasonings, Wood, Cookers, Accessories

Ambrosi Brothers Cutlery

3023 Main St.
Kansas City, MO 64108
(816) 756-3030
http://abcutlery.com/services

Kansas City pitmasters, professional chefs, and home cooks have made Ambrosi Brothers their favorite shop for quality knives, knife sharpening, kitchen equipment, and repairs and maintenance since 1959. Now that his parents, Candido and Esther, are retired, son Alfred owns and runs the business. He was in training for the ownership role since age eight. You'll find a spectrum from high-end cutlery to drawers of used sharpened knives for $1 and up. One of my favorite, most used knives for slicing barbecue meats at home is a wooden-handled chef's knife I bought for $1 at Ambrosi Brothers.

BBQ Addicts
(816) 200-1387
www.bbqaddicts.com/
Online source for ordering the Bacon Explosion, grills and smokers, sauces and rubs, barbecue accessories, fuel, apparel, and gifts.

BBQ Bonanza
737 Kansas Ave.
Kansas City, KS 66105
(913) 281-5111
Purveyor of barbeque cookers, pellets, sauces, rubs, etc.

Garden Complements
920 Cable Rd.
Kansas City, MO 64116
(816) 421-1090
www.gardencomplements.com
Longtime private label barbecue sauce and seasonings producer; now home to Curley's Famous Barbecue Sauces, a legendary award-winning sauce originally fashioned by Curley Atwood in 1955 to serve at Mrs. Atwood's Café in Winfield, Kansas.

Hot Spot Pools, Hot Tubs & BBQ
2101 Kara Ct.
Liberty, MO 64068
(816) 781-8884
www.libertyhottub.com
www.kcbbqsource.com
www.kcxl.com

Kansas Sampler
6858 Johnson Dr.
Mission, KS 66202
(913) 432-3355
921 Massachusetts
Lawrence, KS 66044
(785) 841-1300

4845 W 117th St.
Leawood, KS 66211
(913) 491-3004

9750 Quivira
Lenexa, KS 66215
(913) 396-4240

16485 W 119th St.
Olathe, KS 66061
(913) 390-8090

5918 SW 21st St
Topeka, KS 66604
(785) 273-3066

Original Juan Specialty Foods

111 Southwest Blvd.
Kansas City, KS 66103
(913) 432-5228
www.originaljuan.com

When barbecue sauce and rub entrepreneurs' sales escalate beyond their capacity to keep up with demand, many turn to Original Juan for help. Some of the most popular Kansas City barbecue sauces are made, bottled, labeled, and shipped from Original Juan. Locals and visitors love to stop by for sample tastings and bargains in the outlet store.

Pryde's: Kitchen & Necessities

115 Westport Rd.
Kansas City, MO 64111
(816) 531-5588
www.prydeskitchen.com

Westport, known as Possum Trot to 19th-century westward bound pioneers, has been a longtime Kansas City go-to place for supplies, food, and libations. Pryde's has continued the Westport supplies tradition since 1968. Barbecue lovers dare not miss browsing Pryde's inventory of barbecue sauces, seasonings, cookbooks, gadgets, pots, pans, skillets, grill woks, knives, and the popular ThermoWorks Thermapen. Treat yourself to a slice of Upper Crust Bakery pie or a cookie with a cup of Thou Mayest Kansas City Roasters coffee Friday and Saturday on the lower level. Can't find what you're looking for? Ask Louise

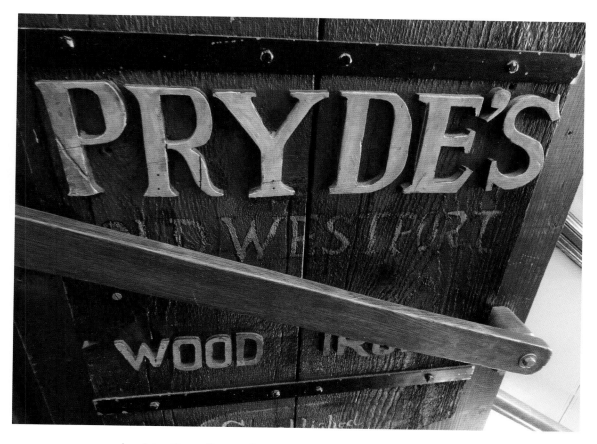

or another friendly staffer. Pryde's Special Blend Coffee or Tea is available during store hours, Monday through Saturday upstairs.

Rally House

18701 E 39th St.
Independence, MO 64057
(816) 994-9080

8650 N Boardwalk Ave.
Kansas City, MO 64154
(816) 888-8400

452 Ward Parkway
Kansas City, MO 64112
(816) 756-5409

Smoke 'n' Fire: Bar-B-Que & Fire-Place

8030 W 151st St.
Overland Park, KS 66223
(913) 685-1111
www.smokenfire.com
Aprons, BBQ accessories, charcoal and pellets, cleaning/care/maintenance, firepits, fireplace, fire starters, flavors, grills and smokers, novelties, smoking wood, planks, and Steven Raichlen: Best of Barbecue products.

The Best of Kansas City

Crown Center Shops
2450 Grand Blvd.,Suite 108
Kansas City, MO 64108
(816) 303-7330
(800) 366-8780
www.thebestofkc.com
BBQ sauces, rubs, books, gift baskets, and more.

The Kansas City BBQ Store

11922 Strang Line Rd.
Olathe, KS 66062
(913) 782-5171

The Best Kansas City Barbecue Sauces

Due largely to the phenomenal nationwide popularity of Dr. Rich Davis' invention, KC Masterpiece® barbecue sauce, Kansas City barbecue sauces are often described as sweet with a tomato base. Many, but not all, Kansas City barbecue sauces fit that description. In fact, three restaurants that have made Kansas City famous for barbecue since the first 50 years of the 20th century—Gates, Rosedale, and Arthur Bryant's—are not sweet. Bryant's original is a vinegar base sauce. Nevertheless, when it says "Kansas City Style" on a barbecue sauce label, whether made in Kansas City or not, odds are that it is sweet with a tomato base.

KC Masterpiece is technically no longer a local brand. It is now under the Kingsford brand and marketed by HV Food Products Company, a subsidiary of the Clorox Company. Since Dr. Davis introduced the original in 1978, new flavors have been added, such as Hickory Brown Sugar, Honey, Hot 'n' Spicy, Smoky Bourbon, and Southern Style, all with the classic KC Masterpiece signature flavor. The 35th Anniversary limited edition, featuring molasses and brown sugar, was released in 2014.

Here's a selection of some of the most popular locally made sauces. As to which is "best": each has a loyal following, and you'll find more than just one of these brands in the pantries and refrigerators of Kansas City's hardcore omnivores. These are some of the Kansas City Barbeque sauces I would recommend:

Arthur Bryant's Barbeque Sauce
www.arthurbryantsbbq.com

Baron of Barbeque Original, Nice & Spicy, Fire & Smoke
www.baron-of-bbq.com

Bigg's Barbeque Sauce Original, Spicy, Sweet Lawrence
www.biggsribs.com

Blues Hog Original
www.blueshog.com

Brobeck's Barbeque Sauce
www.facebook.com/brobecksbbq

Entrepreneurs

Some look at the crowded field of barbecue-related businesses in Kansas City—and the nation, for that matter—and they think, "No way is there room for one more!"

Others survey the scene and see opportunities. Here are examples of a few Kansas City entrepreneurs who saw opportunities and responded successfully to the challenge.

Dr. Rich Davis: Inventor and original producer of the famous American and Kansas City favorite, KC Masterpiece Barbecue Sauce, now owned, produced and distributed by the Kingsford Company. www.kcmasterpiece .com

Gary Berbiglia: Kansas City restaurant owner; former co-owner with Bill Rauschelbach of Arthur Bryant's Barbeque for more than 31 years; currently retired with his wife, Roxane. Gary is a goldmine of knowledge about Kansas City barbecue restaurants and history.

Jack Fiorella: Founder of Fiorella's Jack Stack Barbecue, among the best, most-loved, and most successful barbecue restaurants in the city. Jack's father, Russ Fiorella, founded the former Smokestack BBQ.

Ollie Gates: Co-owner of the family-owned and -operated Gates Bar-B-Q restaurants and some of the most-loved, award-winning barbecue sauces. The Gates name is synonymous with famous Kansas City–style barbecue.

Chef Paul Kirk: World champion barbecue pitmaster, cookbook author, School of Pitmasters founder and teacher, and producer of KC Baron of Barbecue Sauces & Rubs. www.baron-of-bbq.com

Tim Keegan: Director of purchasing/pitmaster at Fiorella's Jack Stack Barbecue; formerly of family-owned Keegan's BBQ. Tim is one of the best pitmasters in Kansas City and America.

Fast Eddy Maurin: Retired KCMO firefighter, barbecue champion, and inventor of a popular line of barbecue cookers for restaurants and competitions, manufactured in Ponca City, Oklahoma, by Cookshack. www.cookshack .com/About-Fast-Eddy

John McDonald: Founder, Boulevard Brewing Company. www.boulevard .com/brewery/our-story

Joe R. Polo Sr.: President/CEO, Original Juan Specialty Foods. www.original juan.com

Jeff & Joy Stehney: Co-owners of three phenomenally popular Joe's Kansas City Bar-B-Que restaurants, plus the KC Barbecue Store, and other enterprises. www.joeskc.com/about, www.thekansascitybbqstore.com/pages/history

Craig & Gay Jones: Savory Addictions, seasoned and smoked artisan nuts. www.savoryaddictions.com

Shannon "Firebug" Kimball: Flavor Trade, an "old school canning and spice company." Makes Firebug barbeque sauces and produces other local artisan sauces for Rib Stars, Uncle Joon's and others, plus hummus and other products. Kimball and business partner Ron Rupp of RQ Barbecue (Shorewood, IL) plan to open a barbecue restaurant in Kansas City. www.flavortrade.com

Danny O'Neill: Owner/Founder of The Roasterie; known in Kansas City as the Bean Baron. The Roasterie brand incorporates coffee into their barbeque sauce, rub, and catsup. www.theroasterie.com

Jason & Megan Day: Burnt Finger Competition Barbecue team, the Bacon Explosion that went viral on the Internet, Burnt Finger Barbecue Sauce and Rub, cookbook—and more. Keep up with Jason and Megan and order their products here: http://blog.bbqaddicts.com/recipes/bacon-explosion

Dan Ulledahl: Barbecue Kansas City LLC. Family man, police officer, and inventor, Dan Ulledahl's "Chop's Power Injector System" is designed to inject liquid seasonings/marinades into meat prior to grilling or smoking. This product took First Place honors, Product of the Year, National Barbecue Association, in 2015. http://barbequekansascity.com

Andy Forbes & Mike Panethere: Royal Barbecue Company. Makers of "The King," a heavy-gauge steel smoker and grill featuring three swing-out grills for smoking or grilling on all three levels. Check their website to find a retailer near you. www.royalbbqcompany.com

Burnt Finger BBQ Sauce Smokey Kansas City Original, Smokey Kansas City Spicy

www.burntfingerbbq.com

Butcher BBQ Sauce

https://www.facebook.com/BurntFingerBBQ

ChickHoovenSwine BBQ Sauce Sweet Caroline, Sweet-n-Heat, Sweet-n-Saucy

www.facebook.com/pages/ChickHoovenSwine-BBQ-Catering/122444177817404

Cowtown Barbeque Sauce Night of the Living Barbeque Sauce

www.cowtownbbq.com

Daniel's

www.danielsbbq.com

Danny Edward's

www.dannyedwardsblvdbbq.com

Dr. Smoke's BBQ Butter

www.throughthesmokebbq.com

Eat Barbecue IPO BBQ Sauce; The Next Big Thing BBQ Sauce

www.eatbarbecue.com

Fat Bastard Hawgwash Barbecue Sauce

No website, but available at online retailers

Fiorella's Jack Stack Barbecue Sauce KC Original, KC Spicy

www.jackstackbbq.com

Fire Bug

www.firebugbbq.com

Four Men & a Pig Barbecue Sauce Original, Spicy

No website, but available at online retailers

Galaxy BBQ Sauce Mild, Solar Heat

www.facebook.com/Galaxy.BBQ.kh

Gates Bar-B-Q Sauce Original Classic, Extra Hot

www.gatesbbq.com

Gluten Free for Men BBQ Sauce

www.glutenfreeformen.com

Grill Side Barbeque Sauce Suburban Sweet

www.grillsidebbq.com/

Hayward's Pit Bar-B-Que Sauce

www.haywards-bbq.com

Heffy's BBQ Sauce Original, Hot & Spicy, Sweet Mesquite

www.heffys.com

Joe's Kansas City Bar-B-Que Sauce

www.joeskc.com

Jon Russell's Kansas City Barbeque Sauce Smokin Ghost, Honey and Spice, Blueberry Habanero, Raspberry Jalapeño

www.jonrussellsbbq.com

Junior's Triple Threat BBQ Sauce

www.facebook.com/TripleThreatBBQSauce

K&M Bar-B-Q Sauce Original, Sweet Heat

www.kandmbbq.com

Kansas City's Finest Barbecue Sauce Classic, Hot

No website, but available at online retailers

LC's Famous Kansas City Barbecue Sauce Mild, Hot

www.facebook.com/pages/LCs-BBQ/186378818079858

Me-Me K's BBQ Sauce

www.me-mekbbq.com

Meat Mitch BBQ Sauce Naked, Whomp

www.meatmitch.com

Plowboys Barbeque Sauce Crossroads, Sweet 180

www.plowboysbbq.com

Quick's Bar-B-Q Original Sauce

https://www.facebook.com/QuicksBBQ

Q39

www.q39kc.com

Barbecue Quirks

Two outstanding Kansas City artists serve as muses to barbecue lovers who take their passion for barbecue way too seriously. Your appreciation of Kansas City–style barbecue is not complete without experiencing the art of Charlie Podrebarac and Mike Savage. Of course, Charlie and Mike can also smoke a mean slab of ribs, and Mike's killer barbecue beans are not to be missed! Catch them at local art shows, galleries, specialty stores, and online.

Cowtown Art by Charlie Podrebarac
www.arttogogo.com/index.htm
Charlie has created enough barbecue-related Cowtown cartoon art to fill at least two books, one of which is already published. His spicy humor surrounds the barbecue snob, purist, and righteous know-it-all lurking inside most Cowtowners and forces us to surrender with guffaws or chuckles.

SavArt – A Simple Gallery
4504 State Line Rd., Kansas City, KS 66103, (913) 236-9400; www.sav-art.com/homepage.php
Mike Savage's bold strokes of color on canvas lend a perspective on Kansas City that is upbeat, familiar, sometimes quirky, and always an invitation to vicariously join the scene. Naturally, Mike's focus often turns to barbecue. Pay attention to details or you'll miss out on some subtle allusions and chuckles. Get Mike's art from his "Simple Gallery" or online.

Barbecue Novels by Kansas City Authors
Mystery novels with a barbecue theme are popular and fun. Thus far the Kansas City barbecue mystery and novel genre belongs to Lou Jane Temple and Doug Worgul.

Revenge of the Barbeque Queens: A Culinary Mystery, Lou Jane Temple (NY: St. Martin's Press, 1997).

Thin Blue Smoke, Doug Worgul (London: Pan Macmillan, 2009).

Rock's Famous BBQ Sauce Tonganoxie

No website, but available at online retailers

Rosedale Bar-B-Q Sauce

www.rosedalebarbeque.com

Rufus Teague Barbecue Sauce Honey Sweet, Blazin' Hot

www.rufusteague.com

Smokin' Guns BBQ Sauce

www.smokingunsbbq.com

Squeal Like A Pig SLAP Sauce

www.facebook.com/SlapsBBQ

Stockyard KC Pitmaster BBQ Sauce Sweet, Red Raspberry

No website, but available at online retailers

Sweet Beaver Barbeque Sauce Original, Hot

www.facebook.com/sweetbeaverbbq

The Roasterie Coffee Barbeque Sauce

www.theroasterie.com

The Sauce Hillsdale Bank Original, Hot

www.hillsdalebankbarbq.com

The Slabs Amazing Glaze Finishing Sauce, Kyle Style Barbecue Sauce

www.theslabs.com

Three Brothers (Different Mothers) Barbecue Sauce Sweet, Spicy

www.threebrothersdifferentmothers.com

Three Little Pigs BBQ Sauce Competition, Kansas City Sweet, Spicy Chipotle

www.three-little-pigs-bbq.com

Woodyard BBQ Sauce

www.woodyardbbq.com

Wyandot BBQ Sauce

www.wyandotbbq.com

OKLAHOMA JOE'S
BAR·B·CUE

- **Jack Daniels:** World Champion Overall
- **American Royal:** Grand Champion Overall
- **World Pork Barbeqlossal:** World Champion Overall
- **American Royal:** Best BBQ Sauce & Rub on the Planet

www.okjoes.com
918-355-0000

Barbecue Contests
in the Metro Area

Kansas City barbecue lovers can enjoy the outdoor sport of barbecue cooking contests from April to October. The 20 contests listed here are sanctioned by the Kansas City Barbeque Society (KCBS). Since contest dates are subject to change, new contests may enter the scene, and contests can be cancelled. Check the KCBS online for up-to-date information at www.kcbs.us/events.php.

April

Smoke on Big Creek BBQ Contest
Pleasant Hill, MO
Benefiting Operation Barbecue Relief
First Friday and Saturday in April
(816) 974-3299
smokinonbigcreek@operationbbqrelief.org
http://smokinonbigcreek.com/

BBQ Challenge
Overland Park, KS
VFW Post 846 BBQ Committee
Third Friday and Saturday in April
Contact: VFW Post 846 BBQ Committee
(913) 648-4991
bbqvfw846@gmail.com
www.bestkcbbq.com

Smokin' in the Ville
Edwardsville, KS
Bonner Springs-Edwardsville Chamber of Commerce
Fourth Friday and Saturday in April
(913) 422-5044
www.bsedwchamber.org/event-1764268

May

Brews, Blues & Bar-B-Q Cookoff

Lansing, KS
First Friday & Saturday in May
Contact: Jessica Waters
(913) 727-5488
cvb@lansing.ks.us
www.lansing.ks.us

Truman Heritage Festival BBQ Championship

First Friday and Saturday in May
Location changes each year; refer to website below
Contact: Sky Smothers
(816) 316-4998
ssmothers@grandview.org
www.grandview.org

Sertoma 48 BBQ

Lawrence, KS
Sertoma Club of Lawrence
Second Friday and Saturday in May
(785) 865-6308
lawrencesertoma@gmail.com
http://lawrencesertoma.com

Kelley Wilson Memorial BBQ Competition

Kansas City, MO
Last Friday and Saturday in May
www.rockhursths.edu

June

Smokin' on the Summit

Lee's Summit, MO
First Friday and Saturday in June
(816) 554-8610
info@smokinonthesummitbbq.com
www.smokinonthesummitbbq.com

Great Lenexa BBQ Battle

Lenexa, KS
Fourth Friday and Saturday in June
Kansas State Championship
(913) 477-7130
lhart@lenexa.com
www.lenexa.com/bbq

July

4th Fest BBQ Contest
Liberty, MO
First weekend in July
(816) 781-5200
gaylep@libertychamber.com
www.liberty4thfest.com

Racing for the BBQ

Lee's Summit, MO
Fourth Friday and Saturday in July
(913) 620-1690
cwhatsoever@yahoo.com
www.racingforthebbq.com

August

BBQ and Fly In on the River

Excelsior Springs, MO
Second Friday and Saturday in August
(816) 519-2113
www.bbqontherivercontest.com

Kansas City Kosher BBQ Competition and Festival

Overland Park, KS
Third Saturday and Sunday in August
(913) 235-6077
www.kckosherbbq.com

Smokin' on Oak

Bonner Springs, KS
Fourth Friday and Saturday in August
www.bsedwchamber.org/event-1764264

September

Leavenworth Hog Wild BBQ Contest

Leavenworth, KS

Second Friday and Saturday in September

www.leavenworthmainstreet.com

Battle of the Brisket

Mission, KS

Third Friday and Saturday in September

www.missioncvb.org/events/battle-of-brisket/

Shawnee Great Grillers State Championship

Shawnee, KS

Fourth Friday and Saturday in September

www.shawneegreatgrillers.com

October

American Royal World Series of Barbecue

Kansas City, MO

First Friday, Saturday, and Sunday in October

Visit www.americanroyal.com for specific date information

Cookin' on the Kaw

DeSoto, KS

Second Friday and Saturday in October

www.desotoks.org

Smoke on the Water

Topeka, KS

Second Friday and Saturday in October

http://parks.snco.us

Barbecue Contests Primer for Spectators

Here's the cruelest reality for spectators at barbecue contests: barbecue every-where, but nary a bone to eat! That is, unless you come prepared. Hence this primer.

When the aroma of meat fires hits your nose, it triggers hunger impulses. You want to eat. You want barbecue. If you haven't been forewarned, you'll feel deflated when a contest official or contestant tells you, "Teams are not allowed to give food to the public." The standard reply from the novice spectator goes something like this: "You mean I went to all the trouble of getting here and there's no free barbecue!?" Add an extra level of anger when admission to the contest grounds is charged.

Now that you're forewarned, here are some tips for having fun and eating barbecue as a spectator at a barbecue contest.

Bring:

Sufficient/appropriate clothing for the weather

Sunglasses

Sunscreen

Cash and credit cards with ID

Mobile phone

A rendezvous plan if you get lost from your companion or group

An event map (mark the teams you especially want to meet or see)

Why can't contestants give free food to spectators at barbecue contests?

Two words explain it: Federal Regulations

I will spare you the technical language. Suffice it to say that it can't be done in the interest of protecting the public health through strict enforcement of safe food-handling procedures.

In most jurisdictions it is the responsibility of county officials to enforce the law. Enforcement varies by county and state, nationwide as well as in the Kansas City metro area. It is best to assume that the strictest rules will be enforced at any given contest. Plan accordingly.

Contest officials know that when you host a barbecue contest and promote it, the public expects to eat barbecue at the event. Here's how they make sure your expectations are met:

Food Vendors

Food vendors who have been inspected and are in compliance with applicable rules and codes are allowed to sell barbecue or other food to the public, often from food trucks.

Teams' Invited Guests

Teams can invite friends, business associates, relatives, or anyone else to enter their designated space. Within the confines of that space, they can share food with guests as they wish. It's the barbecue contest version of friends with benefits.

Judges, Contest Officials, and Volunteers

Judges, officials, and volunteers are selected weeks or months in advance of a contest. Most contest organizers put a priority on selecting Certified Barbecue Judges (CBJs) because most teams prefer to be judged by CBJs who know the rules and are experienced judges.

Don't mistake judging as a ticket for pigging out on free barbecue, however. If you take 1 bite from 6 entries for each of the 4 required KCBS meat categories, it adds up to 24 bites minimum. Depending upon the size of your bites, it could add up to almost a pound—or more. While competition barbecue can be some of the best you've ever eaten, it isn't unheard of for several teams to fall short of excellence on a given day. You could get tough, bitter, creosote-flavored meat, or meat so overpowered with seasonings that you can't taste the meat or natural umami. You aren't likely to get raw meat, but it has happened. Once I judged brisket that tasted fishy. Obviously someone hadn't cleaned the grill after smoking some fish.

Teams usually put enough meat in their entry container to allow leftover meat. Contest officials and volunteers get first dibs at that.

Thus, judging or volunteering is a way to get fed at a contest, but since you earn it, I don't call it "free food."

Several contest sponsors now allow a limited number of contest teams to comply with federal health code regulations and sell contest-style barbecue to the public. It's a win/win arrangement for the public, the vending teams, and the contest sponsor.

Spectator Etiquette

Whether admission is free or not, behave as a guest. Bring and practice your good manners. Politeness is contagious. It is also rewarding. The saw about vinegar repelling and honey attracting may be old, but it is relevant. It works.

Barbecue Cooking Instructors in Kansas City

Upcoming cooking classes are listed monthly in the *KC Bullsheet*. Although the instructors are Kansas City Barbeque Society (KCBS) members, publication in the *Bullsheet* does not imply a KCBS endorsement. Caveat emptor: "Class attendee discretion is advised and encouraged."

Barbecue classes and instructors span the globe. Instructors listed here are based in Kansas City; most are KCBS members in good standing. Contact them directly to sign up for classes locally or in other states/countries. Check with KCBS for classes near you, including classes by KCBS members Myron Mixon, Chris Lilly, Chris Capell, Laura Warner, Rub Bagby, and others.

Baron's School of Pitmasters

Chef Paul Kirk, CWC, PhB, BSAS Certified Working Chef, Doctor of Barbecue Philosophy, Bullshit Artist Supreme
www.baron-of-bbq.com
Chef Paul Kirk, Kansas City Baron of Barbecue and world champion pitmaster, teaches pitmaster classes that cover all of the basics that will make you an expert at home and/or in contests. The curriculum includes tips on meat selection, meat prep, seasonings, sausage making, woods, smoking, and grilling.

The BBQ Queens

www.bbqqueens.com
Karen Adler and Judith Fertig have co-authored a fabulous bunch of barbecue cookbooks. They teach barbecue, grilling, and gourmet cooking classes in Kansas City and all over the world. Contact them at The BBQ Queens website.

Cooking with Shannon

Shannon Firebug Kimball
(816) 868-2154
www.cookingwithshannon.com
Shannon's success at introducing a gourmet line of barbecue sauces and seasonings has attracted a large following of cooks who want to master the barbecue method of cooking, as well as basic and gourmet sides and desserts that complement barbecue meat.

The Culinary Center of Kansas City

Richard McPeake and others
Midwest BBQ Institute
7920 Santa Fe Dr.
Overland Park, KS 66204
(913) 341-4455
www.kcculinary.com/cooking-classes/midwest-bbq-institute
Chef Richard McPeake and the Midwest BBQ Institute faculty cover all aspects of grilling, smoking, sides, desserts, and more with a comprehensive curriculum. Select students form a competition barbecue team and participate in a local barbecue contest—from small contests to the world's largest, American Royal World Series of Barbecue.

Ed Maurin (Fast Eddy Maurin)

(800) 423-0698
www.cookshack.com
Retired firefighter, welder, and champion competition barbecue pitmaster Ed Maurin invented a highly successful line of barbecue pits for commercial or home use in partnership with Cookshack of Ponca City, Oklahoma. Fast Eddy knows fire and barbecue. Sign up for his classes via the Cookshack website or call Cookshack for information.

Lotta BS BBQ

Bob Snelson
242 W Third St.
Prescott, KS. 66767
(913) 471-4669
www.lottabsbbq.com
Longtime Kansas City Barbeque Society member and championship pitmaster, Bob covers all of the barbecue basics for home cooks and competition cooks in his classes. Bob's students master how to pick the best meat, equipment, tools, seasonings, and woods, plus championship smoking and grilling techniques.

Pellet Envy

Rod Gray

(816) 225-1155

www.pelletenvy.com/classes

Rod Gray, head pitmaster, Pellet Envy competition barbecue team, puts his impressive record of barbecue contest wins to work for you in his comprehensive classes on how to win with smoke, fire, and meat. He may even share some secrets he and his wife, Sheri, used on the popular *BBQ Pitmasters* TV series.

Rich and Bunny Tuttle

www.kcassbbq.com

Rich and Bunny Tuttle have competed in and won local and national barbecue cooking contests for several decades. When they are not competing, making their award-winning K-Cass Kick Ass Barbecue Sauce, teaching certified barbecue judging classes, or serving as Kansas City Barbeque Society contest reps locally, in Frisco, Colorado, and elsewhere, they share their championship barbecue secrets in cooking classes. Contact them via their website.

The Rub Bar-B-Que

Dan Janssen

10512 S Ridgeview Rd.

Olathe, KS 66061

(913) 894-1820

http://therubbarbque.com

After you taste the creative barbecue at Chef Dan Janssen's restaurant, The Rub, you may wonder, "How does he do this?" Fortunately, Chef Dan, a Culinary Institute of America graduate, is a skilled teacher as well as learner. Dan offers classes for beginners and for good cooks who aspire to greatness. Most classes focus on a single subject, such as ribs or turkey, brisket, pork, fish, and seafood.

Smoke 'n' Fire – Bar-B-Que & Fire-Place

8030 W 151st St.

Overland Park, KS 66223

(913) 685-1111

www.smokenfire.com

Smoke 'n' Fire hosts a variety of classes featuring local and national barbecue experts. Jim & Joan Cattey and staff also routinely offer friendly in-store guidance and tips on anything barbecue-related.

Three Little Pigs BBQ & Catering

Chris Marks
2450 Grand Blvd.
Kansas City, MO 64108-2535
(816) 421-PIGS [7447]
http://three-little-pigs-bbq.com/classes

Chris Marks comes from a well-known family of barbecue contest champions. He shares his own expertise, along with what he learned over several decades from his father, in classes that focus on ribs and chicken; brisket and butts; tenderloin, beef and pork; turkey and whole chickens; plus a class aimed specifically at how to compete in a barbecue cooking contest. All classes cover basics such as meat selection, seasonings, temperatures, woods, and more. Chris operates the popular Three Little Pigs BBQ & Catering in Kansas City's Crown Center, where his line of award-winning barbecue sauces and rubs are available for sale.

Glossary

You hear lots of jargon in the barbecue network. Below are a few of many terms you may encounter, followed by a brief definition. For more thorough discussions and explanations of most of these terms, I recommend checking with my barbecue buddy, Meathead at www.amazingribs.com.

Barbecue: a method of cooking meat with fire and smoke, either slow and low (smoking) or hot and fast (grilling). Also, meat cooked with fire and smoke. A gathering of people to eat meat cooked with fire and smoke. Slang: main squeeze, as in "struttin' with some barbecue;" sometimes a sexual innuendo, as in "come on over for some barbecue."

Bark: crunchy, flavorful outer crust formed on barbecue meat; a blend of fat, meat, seasonings, and natural umami. Not to be confused with burned sugar caramelized crust.

"Beef & fries": barbecue beef brisket sandwich with French fried potatoes; a frequently ordered combo in Kansas City barbecue restaurants.

Brine: salt in water and/or other liquids such as apple juice, vinegar, or citrus juices, sometimes with added spice or herbal seasonings, used to tenderize meat and add moisture and flavor by way of soaking for several minutes or hours.

Burnt ends: formerly the crusty bark scraps shaved off barbecue briskets. As used today, most meat sold as burnt ends consists of tender, crunchy cubed beef brisket or pork; quality varies by restaurant.

Butt: short for "Boston Butt," the upper portion of a pork shoulder, not from the rear end of a hog.

Carnivores: animals that eat the flesh of other animals, raw or cooked.

DQed: disqualified for non-compliance with one or more contest rules, specifications, or protocol.

Elmer Diller: anthropomorphized term the late John Raven of Texas used to refer to the armadillo, most common in the Southwest. Some have been spotted in south Kansas City.

Hot pit barbecue: meat cooked on grates in pits fueled by hardwood coals beneath the meat in an enclosed steel, brick, or cinder block hot pit.

The Jack: abbreviated term barbecue network people use to refer to the Jack Daniel's World Championship Invitational Barbecue held the fourth weekend in October in Lynchburg, Tennessee, by invitation to qualified teams and judges only.

"Long end" and "Short end": the long end of a pork ribs slab has longer bones and less meat; the short end has shorter bones and more meat.

Money muscle: a piece of muscle on the upper portion of a pork shoulder on the collar, or end opposite from the blade bone; it is shaped like a small tube and is similar in tenderness and flavor to pork tenderloin. Judges love it, thus it helps win money at contests.

Omnivores: animals that eat a variety of meats and produce.

Pelletheads: pitmasters who cook with compressed wood pellet-fueled smokers.

Pellet pooper: slang for a pellet-fueled barbecue pit, alluding to the resemblance of the pellet shapes to small animal droppings.

Perfect judge: derogatory term for one who thinks they know more about how to judge barbecue than anyone else.

Perfect score: when all judges at a judging table give the maximum number of points allowable to a contest entry. In the Kansas City Barbeque Society (KCBS), a perfect score is a total of 180 points and merits special recognition.

Pork butt: the upper portion of the shoulder; sometimes called "Boston Butt," harkening back to a term used by shippers in colonial New England.

Pretty pig: a North Carolina icon for more than half a century, this pig has been barbecued to perfection in every detail. The skin has a golden, brown, or mahogany patina. All body parts are in place with no tears and nothing burned. The meat is tender from head to tail—not tough or mushy. The flavor of a pretty pig is a perfect balance of sweet pig meat complemented with peppered vinegar or mustard and a touch of smoke. Kansas City barbecue restaurants don't routinely serve whole hog, but I've been told that all of the Kansas City barbecued pigs served at catering events are pretty.

"Pulled pork": barbecued pork shoulder so tender that it easily pulls apart in shreds.

Rib sandwich: three to four bone-in sauced pork spareribs between two slices of white sandwich bread.

Rib tips: small, meaty cartilage bone scraps from the breast bone of a slab of pork spareribs that has been trimmed.

The Royal: abbreviated term for the American Royal World Series of Barbecue in Kansas City, the world's largest barbecue contest.

Rub: dry seasonings such as cracked pepper, salt, herbs, and spices, sprinkled or rubbed on raw meat before or after cooking, sometimes both. May also be made into a paste by adding liquids and used for the same purpose.

Shiner: exposed bone on a slab of ribs.

Skunked: placing dead last in a barbecue contest.

Smoke ring: red or pink tint on the outer edge of smoked meats.

Stick burners: pitmasters who cook primarily with pits fueled by hardwood.

"St. Louis cut" ribs: a universally popular rectangular-shaped cut that has become an industry standard. Somebody started a rumor that it was actually invented in Kansas City and copied by so many St. Louis pitmasters that it was named after St. Louis. Historians may yet find the truth.

Yard bird: a chicken; technically, a free-range chicken that eats and roams free in a farmyard.

Index

ABOUT THE AUTHOR

Ardie A. Davis is an iconic member of the barbecue community and a charter member of the Kansas City Barbecue Society as well as an inductee into the KCBS Hall of Flame!

PHOTO BY JIM GREBE